HOUSE
PLANTS

HOUSE PLANTS

ANDY STURGEON

PHOTOGRAPHY BY THOMAS STEWART
STYLING BY LYNDSAY MILNE

conran OCTOPUS

Thanks to Tom and Lyndsay, Muna and Megan, Stephen Reilly, Charlotte Barton for the beginning, Jim Knight at Chessington Nurseries and most of all Sarah, for never giving up hope that I'd eventually finish, and Luke for not making too much noise.

The author and publishers would like to thank the following for allowing us to photograph their homes and premises: Melanie Barnes and Nicholas Nasmyth, John Stevenson, Georgia Sion and Kevin McGuinness, Tom Lloyd and Polly Richards, Adam and Isabelle Sodowick, Anna Malni, Jo Hagan, Kew Gardens, Bow Wow, CA1, Out of Time, Bowles and Linares, Vessel and Palm House Nurseries. Also Sarah Hollywood for the styling on p47, 139, 144 (left) and Christian Siekmeier for the picture of the spider plants on p41.

First published as *Potted* in 2001 by
Conran Octopus Limited
a part of Octopus Publishing Group
2–4 Heron Quays, London E14 4JP
www.conran-octopus.co.uk

Distributed in the United States and Canada by
Sterling Publishing Co.,Inc.
387 Park Avenue South,
New York, NY 10016-8810

This paperback edition published in 2007

Commissioning Editor Claire Wrathall
Senior Editor Muna Reyal
Editor Karen Collier
Creative Director Leslie Harrington
Executive Art Editor Megan Smith
Production Controller Alex Wiltshire
Proofreader Rosie Hankin
Indexer Ingrid Lock

ISBN-10: 1-84091-474-2
ISBN-13: 978-1-84091-474-0

Colour origination by Sang Choy
International, Singapore

Printed in China

CONTENTS

PLANTS ARE GOOD NEWS. THEY'RE GOOD FOR YOUR HEALTH AND GOOD FOR YOUR SOUL. THEY CAN BE COOL, STYLISH, SEXY EVEN, BUT THEY SHOULD BE PART OF YOUR ROOM DESIGN NOT SOME APOLOGETIC AFTERTHOUGHT.

For me the whole gardening thing began with a packet of seeds. Well, to be precise, two packets of seeds, because when I was a child, I grew both kinds. Mustard *and* cress. It starts that way for most people, a small tray on the window-sill, some soggy loo paper and a scattering of seeds. Coming home from school each day to inspect the rapid progress of my miniature field of green ranked right up there with Action Man, Lego and making the stuff they showed us on Blue Peter. Fortunately, I seem to have shaken off the urge to construct space ships from loo rolls and dress male dolls up as soldiers, but the fascination for plants has endured.

Plants are good news. They are good for the environment and good for the soul. Now I don't want to sound like an old hippy, but plants do have an incredibly calming, spiritual effect on people. We use the care of plants as a shield to protect us from our stressful, hectic lifestyles and growing plants either indoors or in the garden satisfies a deep-rooted human instinct to nurture. They're an incredible medicine for both mental and physical health.

Businesses have sussed out the positive effects plants have on people and the spaces they inhabit. They reap the benefits by landscaping their office interiors to increase worker productivity and reduce absenteeism while restaurants and hotels use plants to bring in customers. They invest a lot of money in greenery and not without good reason.

But indoor plants are currently languishing in the midst of a major image crisis which they don't deserve. Unfortunately even the phrase 'house plant' conjures up horrid images of dusty yellow leaves, and sad little spider plants barely clinging onto life, so I won't be using it again.

But where did it all go wrong? We've become obsessed with design and yet we can't get it right in the indoor plant department. Plants should play a vital role in our homes and our places of work. They should be included in the design of a room and not plonked in as an afterthought. A plant should have its own space like a piece of furniture or artwork and be chosen in the same way. Plants with an architectural quality are in vogue, big barrel cacti or graceful trees, but it doesn't end there. The type of container in which it sits is absolutely crucial. Get that wrong and you might as well not bother. A sublime succulent in a grotty plastic pot standing in an old saucer is taboo. After all, it doesn't matter how much you

spend on a dress if you tuck it into the back of your knickers when you come out of the loo.

But, first and foremost, the plants need to be healthy because an ugly plant is worse than no plant at all. The first thing to do is to pick the right plant for the right place and decide on the amount of care you're prepared to give it. Then all you've got to do is keep your plant happy. But as luck would have it, most indoor plants are extraordinarily easy to look after. You just need to follow these five basic rules:

1 Water and feed them correctly. Most indoor plant deaths are caused by overwatering.

2 Most plants need a winter rest with less water, less feeding and less heat.

3 Treat any trouble immediately. Bad doses of pests and diseases are hard to cure.

4 Choose the right plant for the right place. Put it where it grows best not just where it looks best.

5 Avoid extremes or sudden changes in temperature and light.

I've put the common name of each plant first but any one plant can have several different common names. So to clarify this I've also used the Latin name afterwards. Unfortunately a clever bunch of botanists somewhere are constantly renaming plants so your particular plant may be labelled with an obsolete but more familiar moniker. To confuse things even more, some of the big nurseries in Europe have a rather annoying habit of making up their own variety names. What I'm trying to say is don't worry too much about the name of a plant, if it doesn't match up exactly with the one in the book, you're probably quite safe following those care instructions anyway.

The basic tenet of this book is organic. Spraying powerful insecticides indoors is clearly not going to be good for your health or that of your pets so I've offered alternatives. When it comes to organic solutions, there is far less choice in far less fancy packaging because the big chemical companies can't make fat profits out of them, but they do work. And then there are environmental issues like the use of peat which is the main ingredient of most 'off the shelf' indoor plant composts. Peat bogs are ancient habitats and once they are drained are lost for ever. There are plenty of peat-free alternatives on sale and I urge you to use them instead.

Experts now believe that a lot of the stuff we surround ourselves with in our homes and workplaces emits harmful gases. Building materials like plywood, chipboard and paint, carpets, furniture, photocopiers and computers, and the glues and resins that hold them all together give off formaldehyde and all sorts of other nasties. As you are reading this you could be sitting in a self-created haze of 150 horrible things including carbon monoxide, hydrogen, methane, ammonia and nitrogen oxide. To that unpleasant cocktail add low air humidity, exacerbated by heating in winter and we're in all sorts of trouble.

With all that in mind, some experts consider that indoor air pollution is an even greater threat to health than outdoor pollution due to the amount of time we are exposed to it. In our so-called 'advanced societies' we spend a staggering 90 per cent of our lives indoors. Sick Building Syndrome has sidled into our vocabulary and is allegedly responsible for allergies, asthma, eye, nose and throat irritations, fatigue, headaches and respiratory problems.

Good ventilation can improve indoor air quality, but that isn't a realistic option in hermetically sealed office buildings with air conditioning, or even in the home when leaving all the windows open in winter has a rather alarming effect on your heating bills.

Thankfully, in 1980, the good people of NASA started doing extensive research sparked off by the problem of air quality aboard Skylab and they've decided that plants are the answer. After all, in nature, plants clean the atmosphere, and the rainforests are the world's lungs. It's no different indoors. Photosynthesis replenishes the oxygen used up by people, but plants also take in toxins from the atmosphere and break them down with the help of microbes in the compost.

NASA has discovered that some of the best plants are Boston fern, chrysanthemum, gerbera and miniature date palm, but you'll come across details of other excellent air purifiers in this book.

For many people, this book may be the first step of a lengthy gardening odyssey, but for others it could be as far as they'll ever travel on the horticultural road. But however far you journey and no matter how far you've already come, *Potted* should be able to take you wherever you want to go. I don't want this book to be only for flat-dwelling, frustrated gardeners who don't have their own piece of outdoors, I also want it to be useful to people who have no interest in the process of caring for a plant and just want something to look fantastic without any hassle.

I've included lots of plants that are easy to get hold of and easy to look after and I've also included a few new ones that may take a bit of extra trouble and care, but are well worth it. This book will let you dip into it at will and get as little or as much info out as you choose. If you only have one plant then it will tell you how to look after it and maybe, just maybe, encourage you to have more.

MOST PLANTS ARE **INCREDIBLY EASY** TO LOOK AFTER. BUT THE **MAJORITY** ARE **KILLED** BY **OVERWATERING.** **IRONICALLY,** THEY'D DO MUCH BETTER IF **TOTALLY NEGLECTED.**

THE PLANTS

BRIGHT

BRIGHT

In most homes 'bright' translates as 'a window-sill that doesn't get direct midday sunshine' and it is the perfect home for many flowering plants which basically like lots of light all year. If a window is east- or west-facing it will avoid the strongest midday sun, but if it does get direct sunlight it has to be filtered by a translucent blind or a sheer curtain. Or if the sun shines on it all day in summer, you'll need to pull the plant back about 60cm from the glass or there'll be trouble. The healthy greenness can get bleached out of the leaves, dry scorched patches will appear and if you mist them with water they'll discolour. Too far back into the room and the plants won't flower as well and growth gets all leggy. You'll see there are a couple of exceptions here which can benefit from a few hours of direct sunshine, and in winter, when the sun is far less intense, most plants will relish a couple of hours of direct sun a day, which will improve their chances of flowering well.

YESTERDAY, TODAY, TOMORROW PLANT (far left)
Brunfelsia pauciflora/calycina
Slowly reaching about 60cm it flowers in spring and summer. Yesterday the flower was purple, today it's violet and tomorrow it's white. On the fourth day it's had enough and dies. But it will only flower if it has a winter rest.
light bright light, but needs three to four hours of direct sunlight every day in winter.
temperature average warmth except during the winter rest period when it must be moved to a cool room at around 12 or 13°C for six weeks.
water moderately in the summer and feed every two weeks but keep fairly dry in winter.
special needs replace the compost each year but don't increase the pot size, they flower best in small pots. Pinch out the tips to keep it bushy.
problems mealy bug and whitefly.

GOLDFISH PLANT (left)
Columnea x banksii
This one with dark green leaves and red flowers is the easiest variety to grow and, like 'Carnival' (pictured) with red-edged yellow flowers, will bloom nearly all year. All are fairly hard to kill but need a lot of love and affection in order to do well. Cuttings root in four weeks and flower while really young. Put three or four in a pot.
light bright but never direct sun.
temperature average warmth but keep the humidity as high as possible by spraying and standing on a pebble tray.
water moderately. They hate having wet roots. Feed with high-phosphate liquid fertilizer at a quarter of the recommended strength.
special needs every other year trim off the bottom third of the roots with a knife, replace with fresh compost and repot.
problems watch out for aphids.

MADAGASCAR PERIWINKLE
Catharanthus rosea (page 12)
This easy-to-grow plant with shiny green leaves gets covered in pink flowers from mid spring to early autumn. There is a white form 'Albus'. The pharmaceutical trade uses this plant in the fight against childhood leukaemia.
light although bright light is fine, a few hours a day of unadulterated sunshine won't go amiss.
temperature it likes normal room temperatures, but never below 10°C.
water plentifully but don't stand in water and feed with liquid fertilizer every two weeks.
special needs you get really good flowering plants if you grow them from seed in spring.
problems they are best chucked away once they've flowered.

ROSE OF CHINA (page 13)
Hibiscus rosa-sinensis
The trumpet-shaped flowers are outrageously exotic and come in all sorts of colours including white, yellow, pink, orange and crimson. They mostly appear through late spring and summer. Plants happily reach 60cm or more in height.
light a bright window-sill is ideal but a few hours of direct sun each day is appreciated.
temperature average warmth but during the winter move it to somewhere cooler at about 13°C.
water moderately during the active period with a fortnightly high-potash liquid feed. Keep it fairly dry in winter and cut out the feeding.
special needs in spring prune all the stems and branches down to a neat framework about 15cm high.
problems whitefly.

LOLLIPOP PLANT (above)
Pachystachys lutea
It's not to everyone's taste this one. Little white flowers pop out of the lollipop-like cluster of yellow bracts which last for about three months in summer.
light bright filtered light but never direct sun.
temperature Average warmth all the time.
water moderately all year but slightly less in winter.
special needs give a liquid fertilizer every other week from spring to summer.
problems it should flower by the time it reaches 30–40cm. If it doesn't, switch to a high-potash, tomato-type fertilizer.

YELLOW SAGE (left)
Lantana camara

It's a bit of a weed over much of the sub-tropical and tropical world but it looks good indoors. The clusters of tubular flowers open yellow, then turn red. There are forms that have white, orange or pink flowers. Watch out because it's poisonous.

light a few hours of direct sunlight every day all year makes them flower well.

temperature it likes average warmth with a break in winter in a cool room at anything between 5 and 10°C.

water plentifully while in flower with a liquid fertilizer every two weeks and provide high humidity. In winter let it almost dry out.

special needs prune back to about 15cm high in winter. Cuttings taken in spring will flower better than old plants.

problems whitefly.

SHRIMP PLANT
Justicia brandegeeana/ Beloperone guttata

The common name comes from the salmon-coloured sort of prawn-shaped flowers (if you half close your eyes). It's quite common and very easy to grow, flowering for most of the year. An exception to the rule, a sunny window-sill is ideal for this plant, especially if shut behind curtains at night which keeps it nice and cool.

light bright light with a little direct sun.

temperature average warmth, cooler at night.

water moderately, allowing the top to dry out a bit between watering. Water sparingly in winter.

special needs pinch out the tips of young plants to keep bushy. Mature plants can be chopped back by half in mid spring.

problems none in particular.

SILK OAK
Grevillea robusta

This fast-growing tree with fern-like leaves can easily put on 50cm a year if happy. The young leaves are tinged a beautiful coppery brown. They don't flower indoors and are ideal for cool, bright spots.

light bright is best, but they also like direct sun, especially in winter.

temperature cool to average warmth if the humidity is raised.

water moderately in active growth and sparingly in winter.

special needs repot in spring using azalea compost which is acidic. Feed every two weeks from spring to summer.

problems central heating and dry air can make the leaves drop off.

LIPSTICK VINE (right)
Aeschynanthus lobbianus

A long-stemmed trailer with striking red flowers between June and September. Sadly it's a bit temperamental and if you don't give it a proper winter rest it won't flower the following year. Ideal for hanging pots.

light lots of bright light all year but never direct sun.

temperature a room on the cool side of warm is best but they absolutely must have a cooler winter rest at around 13 or 14°C.

water plentifully while in flower and give an extremely weak liquid feed. In winter it's essential to keep it on the dry side. High humidity is a must.

special needs Repot every two or three years.

problems watch out for aphids.

GOOSEFOOT
Syngonium podophyllum

The immature leaves of this tropical vine are shaped like arrowheads but as the plant gets a few years older they develop first two and then four additional pointy lobes. The creamy yellow variegated form 'Emerald Gem' is the most common variety available.

light bright filtered light but absolutely no direct sun which damages the leaves. The green form will grow in medium light but all the variegated ones need bright light or growth slows down and they get a bit leggy.

temperature average warmth with high humidity.

water moderately and sparingly in winter.

special needs liquid feed every two weeks.

problems it may get red spider mite if the air is dry.

Other bright plants *umbrella plant (p80), guatemalan rhubarb (p47/48), dumb-cane (p36/37), begonia (p31)*

DARK

Take a trip down to a flower shop or a garden centre and you'll be faced with all kinds of plants, but sadly most will need to be kept near a window or they'll start to look rubbish several weeks after you get them home. The leaves get a bit lacklustre, the stems get leggy and spindly and the plants will begin a long and painful journey to the other side. Flowering plants are non-starters in dimly lit rooms so foliage plants are the way forward. Nothing will grow in total darkness but the plants here will be ok in the inner recesses of your room away from windows. In the Light and Artificial Light section on page 95 this is described as medium or dim light. Generally they will tolerate bright light as well. You can also use other plants in dim or dark rooms and rotate them by giving them a few weeks on and a month or two off.

DARK

PAINTED DROP-TONGUE
Aglaonema crispum (below left)

This is a brilliant plant for dingy rooms and if you treat it right it will look good for ages. The 30cm long leaves are several shades of green and there are a number of varieties. In summer or early autumn barely noticeable hooded flower spikes appear.

light medium, never direct sun.

temperature average warmth all year. For extra humidity stand on a pebble tray.

water moderately allowing top half to dry out between waterings. It doesn't really have a winter rest. Feed monthly.

special needs repot mature plants once every few years. They never need large pots.

problems cold air and draughts make the leaves curl.

RHUBARB (below right)
Rheum rhaponticum

Rhubarb will actually grow in a windowless room like a hallway. Buy a crown or dig up a lump from the garden in spring. Put it in a big pot and the new leaves will shoot up searching for light.

light doesn't need any, but if it gets some light the leaves will be more green rather than yellow. The pot will need turning so the plant doesn't grow lopsided.

temperature room temperature right down to freezing.

water keep it moist.

special needs plant in soil-based compost with some well-rotted manure. Cut the stems and discard the poisonous leaves. Put it outside in late summer.

problems watch out for aphids on young growth.

IVY TREE
x *Fatshedera lizei*

A cross between ivy and a glossy leaved plant, *Fatsia japonica*. It will grow outside so can put up with cold rooms and entrance halls. The leaves are about 15cm across and shaped like a hand with five pointed fingers. There is a variegated form with cream margins.

light bright or medium light. Variegated forms need the most.

temperature cold is fine. But they will live in heated rooms if the humidity is kept up.

water moderately and then sparingly in winter.

special needs pinch out the tips in spring to keep it bushy. The stems need staking or they'll flop over.

problems watch out for aphids, scale and red spider mite in dry warm air.

PEACE LILY (page 18)
Spathiphyllum 'Mauna Loa'

In spring and summer the 60cm tall clump of glossy green leaves is crowned by a knobbly white flower sheathed in a white spathe. It slowly turns green and lasts about five or six weeks. *S. wallisii* is the more common, smaller variety. Some varieties are fragrant.

light prefers medium light. Too much sun scorches the leaves.

temperature grows well in normal room temperatures, however is sensitive to dry air, so stand pot on a pebble tray. Keep warm and humid to encourage flowering.

water moderately but if you let it dry out, the leaves collapse. Dunk in a bucket of water to revive it. Too wet and the roots rot.

special needs liquid feed every other week from spring to summer.

problems attacks from red spider mite when humidity is low.

PHILODENDRON (page 19)
Philodendron

Philodendrons, which are related to the cheese plant, come in lots of different shapes but most of them have big, lush, glossy leaves. Some of the climbing ones, like the variety 'Red Emerald' have a burgundy tinge to the foliage. *P. selloum* and *P. bipinnatifidum* make a massive clump of huge deeply lobed leaves and are probably a bit big for the average room.

light actually prefer bright light, but do grow well in darker corners. If the leaves become small and pale, move towards the window.

temperature average warmth, never below 14°C.

water moderately, just enough to keep soil moist. In the winter, let compost dry out.

special needs use a moss-covered pole to support climbers, spray the moss daily with water and poke the aerial roots into it.

problems yellow leaves are caused by overwatering.

PARLOUR PALM (above)
Chamaedorea elegans

This slow-growing palm will eventually reach about 90cm and is virtually indestructible. After about three years sprays of small bobbly yellow flowers appear.

light grows well in anything from dim to bright light.

temperature tolerates a wide range, but does best in normal room temperatures. Can stomach dry air but becomes prone to red spider mite and brown leaf tips.

water plentifully during the active period to keep the compost moist. In winter keep it barely moist.

special needs give a liquid feed once a month during spring and summer.

problems yellowing, mottled leaves are probably caused by red spider mite.

CARDOMOM
Elettaria cardomomum

Probably not the prettiest plant in the world, but its ability to thrive in extremely poor light makes it very useful. If you can't get anything else to grow try this. The pointed leaves are over 30cm long on stalks as high as 75cm. Flowers rarely appear indoors. The leaves are aromatic if crushed.

light very poor to bright light. Can survive anything except direct sunlight.

temperature average warmth.

water moderately in active growth and sparingly in winter. Liquid feed every other week.

special needs to propagate, clumps can be divided or it can be grown from seed.

problems leaf edges turn brown if it's too cold.

Other dark plants *prayer plant (p32), goosefoot – green (p16), ivy (p53), cast iron plant (p71)*

WARM

Most popular indoor plants are only popular because they like the same sort of living conditions as we do. But this can cause a few problems for anyone who likes to set the thermostat on their heating a little higher than normal because a lot of plants won't like it. The plants in this category won't mind those few extra degrees, but the golden rule is: the hotter the room, the higher the humidity must be. In most cases standing pots on a layer of pebbles in a saucer of water will do the trick. As the water evaporates, the humidity around the plant is increased, but the pot mustn't actually be in the water. Standing a container of water on a radiator near the plants also makes a difference.

DIPLADENIA (page 22)
Mandevilla sanderi

This is really a twining climber but it flowers when it's quite young, which is a bonus. The trumpet-shaped blooms are pink with a yellow throat and some are almost red, and last from late spring to early autumn. The glossy green leaves remain all year.

light bright light is essential. Direct sunlight will damage it, but too little light and it won't flower.

temperature average warmth but it needs a cooler rest period in winter. Keep the humidity up.

water sparingly and keep slightly drier in winter.

special needs liquid feed every two weeks in active growth.

problems they only flower on the current year's growth so once the blooms have finished, trim back all this growth to the main stems.

GOODLUCK PLANT (left)
Cordyline fruticosa

Cordylines and dracaenas are very similar and need roughly the same conditions. This one with red-splashed leaves grows to about 60cm tall. It develops a bit of a cane as the lower leaves yellow and naturally drop off.

light bright light. Direct sun bleaches dry patches in the leaves.

temperature average warmth or warm rooms but you must raise the humidity.

water plentiful with a liquid feed every two weeks, but ease off in winter or you'll kill it. Severe underwatering causes brown spots.

propagation propagate with cane cuttings in spring.

problems it will die in cold rooms.

VELVET PLANT (page 23)
Gynura sarmentosa

Aptly named, the hairy leaves of this little trailing plant are iridescent and shimmer in a peacock's tail-sort-of-way.

light give bright light, with some direct sunlight.

temperature average warmth is fine but they'll grow in warm rooms as long as you stand in a pebble tray to raise the humidity.

water moderately in active period, do not wet the foliage. Liquid feed once a month except in winter.

special needs nip out the tips to keep it bushy and remove the small revolting-smelling dandelion-like flowers in spring.

problems watch out for aphids.

SILVER NET LEAF (right)
Fittonia verschaffeltii argyroneura

This plant has a nasty habit of kicking the bucket a couple of weeks after you've got it home. The solution to this is lots of warmth and humidity around the leaves. The dwarf varieties are strangely easier to grow. The most common type with pink veining is a little tasteless.

light medium light in summer but move to a brighter place in winter.

temperature quite warm is best, but watch the humidity.

water little and often is best with a liquid feed every other week. Keep the compost just moist and let it get a bit drier in winter.

special needs plants get straggly so trim them back in spring.

problems if it gets a bit cold or the compost ever dries out, the plant is history.

EMERALD TREE (below)
Radermachera sinica

What sets this plant apart from the others is its tolerance of dry air and therefore centrally heated rooms. Otherwise it has to be said that despite its elegant name this plant is not much of a looker. It just sort of grows into a small green tree but people seem to like it.

light bright but detests midday summer sun.

temperature likes average warmth, but it will be happy in quite warm rooms.

water plentifully but don't let it get soggy.

special needs feed every other week in active growth. Propagate with stem cuttings in the summer.

problems none really, but very occasionally whitefly.

ANGEL'S WINGS
Caladium hortulanum

Papery thin, arrow-shaped leaves about 40cm long rise up on stalks of the same length between late spring and autumn. These spectacular plants may be white with green veining or marbled red, pink or green. Because they need unusually high temperatures and humidity they are best treated as temporary plants but they can be kept and brought back into leaf the following year.

light bright light but not direct sun.

temperature above average warmth with a very high humidity.

water moderately but as the leaves die down reduce watering and keep fairly dry for about five months. Liquid feed at half strength every other week.

special needs use a peat substitute compost.

problems leaves go brown and dry if humidity is too low.

TEMPLE BELLS
Smithiantha

The dangling bell-like flowers in late autumn may be orange or red, often with a speckled yellow throat depending on which variety you have. The heart-shaped leaves have a curious mottling and plants themselves can be around 60cm tall. They have a completely dormant winter rest.

light medium to bright light away from direct sun.

temperature warm and humid. Don't let it drop below about 18ºC. Conservatories are best.

water moderately to keep it moist except in winter rest period.

special needs after flowering the plants die down. Let the compost dry out and remove the short scaly brown rhizomes from the pot and store in vermiculite until repotted in spring.

problems brown leaves are caused by dry heat and overwatering.

WARM

FALSE ARALIA (below left)
*Schefflera elegantissima/
Dizygotheca elegantissima*
Check out any film or TV show
that was made before about 1995
that featured cannabis plants and
you can bet that it was actually this
or its stumpier-leaved cousin, often
sold as *D. veitchii*. In fact, the
almost black leaves are far too
dark, but that never seemed to
bother anyone.
light bright but never direct sun.
temperature warmth is absolutely
vital. So is humidity.
water sparingly, but it walks a very
thin line between over- and underwatering. Give little and often.
special needs being slow-growing
they only need moving into a
larger pot every other year. Put
three plants per pot to make them
look bushier.
problems leaf drop is caused by
cold, underwatering and sudden
changes in temperature.

CALATHEA (below right)
Burle-marxii
These plants are very closely
related to ctenanthes and can be
a little petulant but the leaves have
amazing patterns which makes
them worth it.
light bright light. Direct sun curls
the leaves.
temperature keep it warm, at
least 20ºC and preferably higher.
Keep the humidity up.
water moderately to keep it moist
and then sparingly in winter. Don't
use cold or hard water. Feed every
two weeks in spring and summer.
special needs never feed until at
least four months after repotting.
problems stems go limp and rot if
plants are too cold or overwatered
in winter.

MONKEY PLANT
Ruellia makoyana
The velvety green leaves have a
tinge of purple and silver veining,
and in winter it has 5cm long rose
pink trumpet flowers. The stems
tend to flop making it a good plant
for a hanging basket.
light bright light, especially in the
winter months or else flowering
period is shortened.
temperature must be kept warm
with a high humidity.
water moderately but give them
a two-month rest after flowering
and only water sparingly.
special needs repot if necessary
in spring.
problems watch out for aphids on
the shoot tips.

Other warm plants *kris plant
(p78), glory lily (p163/165),
bromeliads (p132–135),
allamanda (p164)*

COOL

If you've got somewhere in your home that gets a bit chilly, you may have trouble growing a lot of the usual indoor plants. The trick is to choose tough things that don't mind the lack of warmth. These plants are particularly useful for barely heated or seldom-used rooms, communal stairwells and corridors, porches and even cool conservatories. Just remember that they like cool not cold, so most won't appreciate freezing conditions.

PORCELAIN BERRY (page 28 left)
Ampelopsis brevipedunculata
'Elegans'
Normally sold as an outdoor plant, this little climber has green leaves splashed white and pink with pinky red stems. It can be trained as a climber or left to trail.
light bright filtered light is essential.
temperature cold and unheated rooms are best but will grow in ordinary room temperatures.
water moderately. Never let it dry out. Sparingly in winter.
special needs prune at any time of year to keep it to a manageable size and to stop it from getting straggly.
problems too much humidity can encourage mildew.

GUM TREE (page 28 right + 29)
Eucalyptus
There are many different varieties; just choose one that looks good when it's young. Cool bright rooms like unheated stairwells are ideal. Some can also be used as temporary indoor plants and put outside after a month or two.
light as much as possible.
temperature they grow best in cool rooms. Average room temperatures can make them go crispy after a short while.
water moderately with a fortnightly liquid feed. Water sparingly in winter.
special needs might need some pruning to make it bushy rather than tall and thin.
problems they will only last a year or two at most indoors.

FLOWERING MAPLE (below)
Abutilon x *hybridum*
These shrubby plants can be anything up to about 1.5m, but flower when quite young in white, yellow, red and orange. There are also some with variegated leaves splashed with yellow. It is happy as an indoor plant or in a cool greenhouse or conservatory.
light bright with at least three to four hours of direct sunlight.
temperature a cool room. The warmer it is the higher the humidity needs to be.
water moderately, keep quite dry in winter. Liquid feed fortnightly in spring and summer.
special needs may become tall and spindly so cut back to about 30cm in early spring.
problems whitefly, greenfly and red spider mite.

BEGONIA (below)
Begonia
There are loads of different begonias, some grown for their outrageously gaudy leaves, some for their pretty flowers and others (which make the best indoor plants) for both. There are tiny ones and huge climbing ones too numerous to mention.
light a bright spot but no direct sun except in the depths of winter.
temperature no higher than 20°C. Avoid really cold nights. Keep humidity high during the growth period.
water moderately while active and feed every two weeks. Water sparingly in winter. Begonias hate overwatering.
special needs repot foliage types every spring or they'll lose colour.
problems rots and mildews.

CAPE COWSLIP
Lachenalia aloides
This is a beautiful plant but unfortunately can't live in heated rooms. The speckled green strap-like leaves arise from a bulb which flowers in winter. Small hanging bells of yellow flowers that fade to scarlet at the tips are carried on stalks about 30cm tall.
light bright with some direct sun.
temperature really cool, as low as 5°C in winter.
water moderately, keeping moist while in flower.
special needs slow down watering after flowering and stop after about a month. Keep it dry and repot in autumn. Start watering once shoots appear.
problems warm rooms are a killer.

GENISTA
Genista x spachiana
You'll see these small bushes for sale in spring and early summer. Yellow, slightly fragrant pea-like flowers virtually obscure the thin pale green leaves. They really are temporary plants that look rubbish for 11 months of the year, so chuck them after flowering.
light bright with some sunlight.
temperature cool rooms make the flowers last for much longer.
water plentifully before and during flowering.
special needs if you really want to keep them, cut back the shoots after flowering, stand outside and then bring into a cool room in autumn. Increase the watering in mid winter.
problems only what they look like for most of the year.

COOL

ROSE (left)
Rosa chinensis

Often known as miniature roses or patio roses, these are the only ones suitable for indoors. They are about 30cm tall, usually flower between early spring and autumn, come in a range of colours, but are rarely scented. Some people keep them all year but they should be put in the garden once they are past their best or chucked away.
light bright light.
temperature cool window-sills are best, but they will be happy in ordinary room temperatures.
water moderately and never let it dry out. Liquid feed once every two weeks.
special needs prune by half in early spring before bringing them back indoors. Deadhead regularly.
problems watch out for aphids and red spider mite.

KAFFIR LILY
Clivia miniata

Dark green strap-shaped leaves, as much as 7cm wide, fan out from the centre and plants can be 90cm across. In late winter a flower spike about 45cm tall pushes up from near the middle of the plant. Yellow-tinged orange bell-shaped flowers open at the top.
light bright light but no direct sun.
temperature they need a cool, preferably unheated, room for about two months in winter but are happy in average warmth while actively growing.
water moderately from spring to autumn and then sparingly, just enough so it doesn't dry out.
special needs liquid feed every two weeks from when the flower stalks start showing until early autumn. Only repot if it's bursting out of its pot. Remove seed pods after flowering.
problems too much winter warmth causes small, short, early flowers.

PRAYER PLANT
Maranta leuconeura kerchoveana

The common name comes from this little plant's nocturnal habit of curling its leaves up and raising them to the heavens. The pale green foliage has dark brown blotches either side of the mid rib.
light medium light. Strong light browns the edges and leaves fade.
temperature it only just sneaks into this category because it really prefers cool bordering on warm, but definitely not cold. Anything between about 18 and 21°C is good, any higher and the humidity must be increased.
water plentifully, but sparingly in winter.
special needs propagate by dividing clumps in spring. Feed every two weeks in active growth.
problems stems go limp if plants get too cold.

LADY'S EARDROPS (right)
Fuchsia

There are thousands of varieties, most of which have these pod-like flower buds. You can either buy small plants in spring and discard them after flowering or you can overwinter the plants somewhere very cool and put them back on show in spring.
light bright light, with a couple hours of strong sunlight every day.
temperature likes cool conditions.
water plentifully but in winter keep fairly dry. Feed every week when in flower.
special needs in spring trim back by a third. Take cuttings in late summer or spring.
problems attacks from aphids and whitefly.

Other cool plants *rhubarb (p20) cape leadwort (p53), buddhist pine (p59), lapageria (p164), oleander (p164)*

'Ostentatious, art of worthless pretentiousness' is the dictionary definition for kitsch and these plants definitely fit the bill. Ostentatious without a doubt, some people would consider them so gaudy and tasteless as to also be completely worthless but they have their admirers. Many seem to belong to another time and are for ever trapped in a previous decade, but they all have a certain something. It's just hard to figure out what it is.

KITSCH

KITSCH

HERRINGBONE PLANT
Maranta leuconeura var. *erythroneura* (below left)
The unbelievably exotic leaves are a luxurious deep velvety green with pink herringbone veins and paler green markings. Underneath they are a purple colour.
light medium light, but in the winter give them a well-lit, sunless spot. Too much light gives the leaves brown edges.
temperature it likes average warmth, but keep the humidity up by standing the pots on moist pebbles.
water plenty in the active months, less in winter. Avoid splashing the leaves.
special needs liquid feed once every two weeks. Repot in spring.
problems sensitive to direct sunlight and dislikes draughts with a passion.

SWISS CHEESE PLANT
Monstera deliciosa (below right)
There can't be many people who don't know this plant. The mature leaves can be 60cm across with lots of holes and perforations but in normal room conditions they stay on the smaller side. Like many philodendrons, they naturally grow up tree trunks so need some sort of support.
light bright to fairly dim conditions.
temperature average warmth, keep the humidity up if you can.
water moderately during active growth and sparingly in winter. Overwatering turns leaves yellow.
special needs liquid feed once every two weeks during active period. Repot in spring.
problems not enough light causes leggy growth and leaves without holes. Dry air causes brown leaf tips.

DUMB-CANE (right)
Dieffenbachia amoena
The big leaves are splashed with a creamy white and the plant can get to 1.5m in height, but as it ages the lower leaves naturally fall to reveal a cane. *D. Seguine* 'Tropic Snow' is a particularly good one and there are smaller clumpier varieties like *D. picta* 'Camilla'. These plants are toxic and in their native South America the men of certain tribes brew a potion which freezes the vocal chords of their womenfolk. Hence dumb-cane. It's also a good air purifier.
light bright filtered light. Direct sun bleaches leaves.
temperature warm conditions, it doesn't like cold rooms at all. High humidity is important.
water moderately and then sparingly in winter.
special points feed every two weeks with liquid feed in its active period.
problems cold and draughts make lower leaves yellow and wilt. Watch out for red spider mite and wash your hands after touching it as the plant is poisonous.

COCKSCOMB/PLUME FLOWER
Celosia
Usually grown outside as a bedding plant, there are two types. One, *C. argentea* var. *cristata*, has colourful velvety cockscomb flowers that look totally artificial and the other, with spiky, fluffy plumes, is *C. Plumosa* group. They both come in reds, pinks and yellows.
light lots of light but be sure to avoid baking sun.
temperature cool temperatures make the flowers last longer.
water moderately, keeping the compost always moist.
special needs buy in bud or flower, keep on a window-sill and chuck out after flowering.
problems none really.

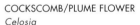

URN PLANT (page 34 + 35)
Aechmea fasciata
This bromeliad has thick leathery grey leaves with a whitish bloom which smudges if touched. The gaudy pink flower head is actually made up of bracts or modified leaves and lasts for six months.
light growth in full sunlight is essential for flowering.
temperature average warmth with high humidity.
water keep the central vase topped up with water, refresh it every few weeks. Water the compost moderately and let it dry a bit between waterings. Feed with half-strength liquid feed every other week while active.
special needs trim away parent plant after flowering and allow offsets to develop.
problems parent plants die off after flowering.

CHENILLE PLANT
Acalypha hispida
There are two types: those with 45cm long tassels of tiny bright red flowers in late summer and autumn, and those grown for their patterned leaves mottled coppery green and streaked with red and purple. The flowering sort are definitely the most kitsch with their funny rat-tail flowers. In a conservatory, both plants can reach the height of a person.
light bright light.
temperature always warm but with a high humidity.
water plentifully and then sparingly in winter.
special needs they branch naturally; pruning will only remove flower buds.
problems watch out for mealy bug and red spider mite especially in dry air.

CALATHEA (above)
Calathea crocata
Most calatheas are grown for their colourful leaves but this one has curious orange flowers on erect stems. The dark green leaves have a purple tinge beneath and make a neat clump about 40cm high.
light medium. Bright light tends to spoil the leaf colouring.
temperature average warmth with good humidity.
water plentifully during the active growing period, but go easy during the rest period.
special needs a liquid feed every other week is important during active growth.
problems limp stems are caused by cold air and wet compost in winter months.

KITSCH

TUBEROUS BEGONIAS
Begonia (below left)

These plants are temporary visitors which make a splash of colour and then die back down. They flower in summer and autumn and are bought in bloom or raised by planting the tubers (the knobbly rooty things) in spring in moist compost.

light bright light is essential.
temperature average warmth, store somewhere cool in winter.
water freely when in flower but keep the tubers dry in winter.
special needs after flowering, withhold water and cut off shoots. Lift tubers and store in compost.
problems non-tuberous types can be chucked after flowering.

CAPE PRIMROSE (below right)
Streptocarpus

There are all kinds of varieties and colours of this little plant. The crinkly green leaves just sort of sit there not doing much but they flower almost non-stop. There are some extraordinarily beautiful types like *S. pentherianus* which have only one large leaf.

light bright light when active and medium light in the winter.
temperature average warmth. Raise humidity in warm rooms.
water moderately when active and sparingly in winter especially if there is a non-flowering rest period.
special needs apply a high-phosphate liquid feed at half strength every two weeks in the active period. Remove seed pods and flowers as they fade to encourage further blooms.
problems avoid cold draughts. Single-leaved types normally die after flowering.

COCK ON A PLATE (right)
Anthurium scherzerianum

Not the easiest plant to grow but well worth it. The waxy red 'flowers' with their flower spikes appear between spring and late summer and last for some time. They have dark green leathery leaves. There are also white and pink varieties.

light medium light, put them near a slightly shaded window.
temperature average warmth. Keep humidity levels up to encourage flowering.
water plentifully when active but sparingly in winter.
special needs liquid feed every two weeks in spring and summer.
problems dislikes fluctuations in air temperature. Leaves get dusty.

Other kitsch plants *croton, flame nettle, zebra plant and devil's ivy (all p44)*

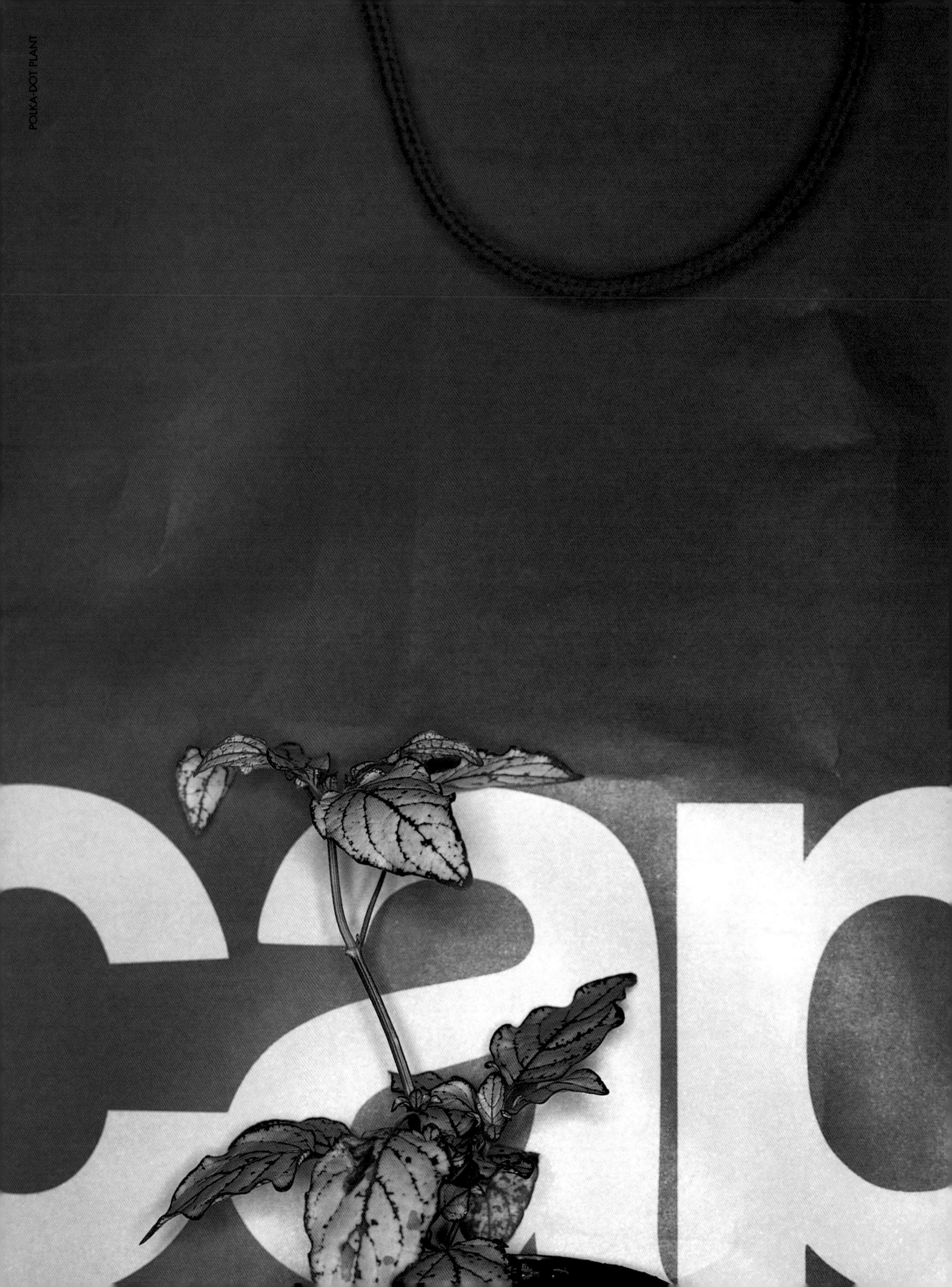

POLKA-DOT PLANT

PARIAHS

Some plants are unquestionably vile. Laws should be passed to prevent their sale in the shops and they should be made unwelcome in our homes. There are plenty to choose from: brash gaudy things that totally lack style and plain ugly things without any obvious merits. Many were popular in a bygone era and quite frankly should have been left there. But, of course, fashion goes in circles and it's inevitable that today's pariahs will become tomorrow's essentials. So what you'll see here is an indictment of the past and doubtless a prediction for the future.

REX BEGONIA (above left)
Begonia rex 'Vesuvius'
These foliage begonias come in a veritable rainbow of colours – extraordinary combinations of pinks, gold, yellows and anything else you can think of. To add insult to injury they sort of shimmer which makes them also look totally artificial.
light bright light, but never direct sun. Turn the pots occasionally.
temperature average warmth but never below about 15°C. They like high humidity.
water moist from spring to autumn and then sparingly in the winter months.
special needs propagation is unfortunately very easy from leaf cuttings.
problems pot-bound plants lose their colour.

RUBBER PLANT (above right)
Ficus elastica 'Decora'
The problem with rubber plants is that they just grow straight up so you end up with a tall thin plant that's bashing its head on the ceiling. They were real seventies' plants and went hand in hand with the rest of the awful fashions of that decade. The variegated ones, like 'Tricolor' which is splashed with pink and cream, are particularly unpleasant.
light dingy rooms make them a bit leggy but they do seem able to grow anywhere.
temperature again not fussy.
water keep it fairly dry.
special needs air layering is your best bet for propagation.
problems overwatering will cause lower leaves to fall. The leaves get very dusty.

PEPPER ELDER
(below left and right)
Peperomia caperata 'Red Luna'
You're probably wondering why this is here because it does look rather good. The heart-shaped leaves and rat-tail flowers add up to a stylish little 10cm plant so what's the problem? The problem is that it rapidly dies, but not before losing its leaves and becoming very ugly.
light bright, but shade from sun.
temperature average warmth, but if it's too warm they'll lose their leaves unless the humidity is raised.
water compost must dry a little between waterings, cut right down in winter, use tepid water and don't get it on the leaves.
special needs propagate in spring with 5–7cm tip cuttings or try your hand at leaf cuttings.
problems cold makes the leaves drop off, overwatering makes leaves wilt and stems rot, and draughts cause brown leaf edges.

POLKA-DOT PLANT (page 40)
Hypoestes phyllostachya
Most varieties of this objectionable little thing have spots of pink like someone's spilt a can of paint. There's one called 'Splash' which is particularly nasty. On top of that, they tend to get straggly with age.
light bright filtered light.
temperature average warmth, slightly cooler in winter.
water moderately, keep the compost just moist and feed every two weeks in active growth. If it dries out, the plant may die. Oh well.
special needs propagate by taking 10cm cuttings, remove the lower leaves and root them in a glass of water.
problems they aren't as easy to kill as they should be.

AFRICAN VIOLET (page 41)
Saintpaulia ionantha
These are old people's plants. When you reach a certain age you get a bus pass, a pension and an African violet.
light a bright window-sill. They won't flower if they don't get enough light in winter.
temperature like their owners they need a nice warm room and don't like draughts. They love high humidity.
water moderately. Too much water makes the roots rot. Use tepid water and don't get it on the leaves or they'll get brown spots. At every watering give a one-quarter strength liquid feed during active growth.
special needs take leaf cuttings for propagation.
problems apart from generally being horrid, they can get mealy bugs, aphids and botrytis.

DEVIL'S IVY

Epipremnum aureum/
Scindapsus aureus

Perhaps its only saving grace is its ability to purify air. A climber or trailer, it can grow several metres or more. The usual form has bright green, heart-shaped leaves splashed with yellow, but there are others with white marbling. All look artificial. People really love this ugly plant, perhaps because it's easy to grow. They seem to do really well in chip shops.

light bright filtered light.

temperature average warmth.

water moderately during active growth and just enough in winter to stop it drying out.

special needs liquid feed every two weeks. Repot, if necessary, each spring. Pinch out tips to keep bushy.

problems in low light levels, leaf colour fades. Avoid draughts.

CROTON (right)

Codiaeum variegatum var. *pictum*

The one pictured is possibly the most acceptable form of this plant. Most of the others have broader leathery leaves with all kinds of spots and blotches in red, orange and yellow, often all at once. They look like plastic.

light lots of light is essential on an east- or west-facing window, otherwise you get leaf loss and poor colour.

temperature average warmth with a high humidity.

water plentifully, but go easy in winter. Liquid feed every two weeks from spring to autumn.

special needs move into a pot one size bigger each spring.

problems red spider mite and scale may cause problems. Brown leaf edges are caused by low temperatures.

BUSY LIZZIE (above)

Impatiens walleriana

There are plenty of these plants in our gardens so there's no need to bring them inside as well. Some have vivid pink or red flowers and then there are the New Guinea hybrids with splashes of yellow on the leaves. They tend to become leggy, lose their leaves and flowers and develop stem rots. All in all, they're remarkably fussy indoors.

light lots of bright light.

temperature average warmth.

water keep it moist, water a little almost every day in summer. Liquid feed every two weeks.

special needs they won't flower when you repot them.

problems avoid hot dry air, too much light, too little light, overwatering and underwatering.

FLAME NETTLE

Coleus/Plectranthus

Brighter leaves and a greater range of colours is probably impossible to find. But why even look? They all have the appearance of the aftermath of a technicolor yawn or some bad psychedelic experience. In their defence they are quick and easy to grow and make bushes 30–60cm high. They are often used outside for bedding.

light as much as possible, including some full sun.

temperature average warmth but raise the humidity in higher temperatures.

water plentifully. Plants quickly wilt if they're too dry and although they virtually recover they will then shed a few leaves.

special needs regularly nip out the growing tips to keep them bushy and never let them flower.

problems watch out for red spider mite in dry rooms.

ZEBRA PLANT

Aphelandra squarrosa

The zebra plant could also have gone into Kitsch because it looks the part, but it's hard to care for so really does belong here. The glossy green leaves with startling ivory markings are about 20cm long and in spring there are cone-shaped flower spikes of yellow bracts. The plants reach about 40cm high.

light bright light.

temperature average warmth with high humidity.

water plentifully in active growth and barely moist in winter.

special needs these greedy plants need liquid feed every week while in growth.

problems leaves always seem to fall off as a result of underwatering, cold air, draughts or too much sun. It's really hard to get them to flower again. Watch out for aphids, mealy bug and scale at the shoot tips.

Other pariahs *none because they are intentionally left out.*

PLAIN PECULIAR

Some plants look weird. They just aren't what we expect and don't conform to our image of what an indoor plant is: pretty flowers, perhaps some heart-shaped leaves and maybe a nice trunk. There are probably many other plants in these pages that could fall into this category but these ones are definitely quite odd or just not usually grown as indoor plants.

PLAIN PECULIAR

SAGO PALM (far left)
Cycas revoluta
Like a palm but not a palm, this plant was around when the dinosaurs roamed the earth. Very slow growing, it may only put on one stiff green leaf a year and lives for ages. It won't flower indoors.
light give them loads of bright light with or without direct sun.
temperature average warmth. It will tolerate a range of temperatures and low humidity.
water moderately in summer and in the winter only enough to stop compost from drying out.
special needs liquid feed monthly from early spring to early autumn.
problems too much water will eventually kill the plant.

DEVIL'S ROOT (left)
Zamioculcas zamiifolia
This succulent has shiny fleshy stems and leaves that look like they've come out of a mould.
light bright or direct sunlight.
temperature average warmth.
water moderately, sparingly in winter. Overwatering tends to rot the roots and the base of the stem.
special needs liquid feed every other week in active growth.
problems very easy to keep with enough light. Don't overwater.

TURF (GRASS)
An ordinary piece of turf makes an unusual indoor plant. Cut it into strips or any shape you want and put in containers on the window-sill. It can also be easily grown from a thin scattering of seed.
light bright or full sunlight is essential. Turn the container round every day so it doesn't grow bendy.
temperature cold to average. The warmer it is the faster it will grow.
water plentifully. Keep moist.
special needs feeding isn't necessary. Grow in shallow trays or pots with 3 or 4cm of compost. Trim once or twice a week.
problems watch out for mould and spray with a fungicide.

BEAD PLANT (page 46)
Nertera granadensis
This plant used to be very fashionable but its 1970s' appeal left it on the style scrap heap. Watch out because it's due for a comeback. A low mat of creeping green leaves is covered in orange berries the size of small peas. They are fully developed by late summer and last a few months.
light bright light with at least three hours of direct sunlight every day.
temperature cool to average warmth. Keep humidity high.
water moderately, just enough in winter so it doesn't dry out.
special needs put outside in late spring if you can until the berries start to form. Liquid feed now and then during the summer.
problems not always worth coaxing back into 'berry', it is often binned afterwards.

GUATEMALAN RHUBARB
Jatropha podagrica (page 47)
A weirdo of a plant from Central America, the swollen bottle stem is naked in winter but in early spring, flower stalks appear and are topped by tiny coral-red flowers which last for ages. Several deeply lobed leaves will appear later which the Mayans boil and eat. *J. curcas*, a close relative, was used for high-octane fuel trials in Sri Lanka. Reaches about 60cm tall.
light bright light. Avoid direct summer sun.
temperature average warmth.
water sparingly with very little in winter. Overwatering leads to blackened shoot tips.
special needs when necessary, repot in spring or the lower leaves will yellow or drop in summer.
problems mealy bugs.

MALABAR NIGHTSHADE
Basella rubra (this page)
This twining climber with waxy green, purple-tinged leaves is probably best in a conservatory, but it will grow in a bright room. The pink and white flower buds on the shoot tips never really open and just swell to form small black berries. It grows over a metre a year.
light bright filtered light and even a little direct sunshine. Put outside in summer if you can.
temperature average warmth.
water plentifully in active growth and then cut right down in winter.
special needs liquid feed every two or three weeks in active growth. Cut back at any time if growth is excessive.
problems none in particular.

INDOOR BONSAI
All the best sorts have to be kept outside but there are a few fairly decent ones grown from familiar indoor plants. The older the plant, the more expensive it is, but some of the ones for sale are basically just tree seedlings so watch out. Look up the growing conditions for the particular plant but here's a basic guideline.
light bright light.
temperature average warmth.
water always moist but not wet, this can mean a daily soaking. Humidity is important.
special needs continually pinch out the growing tips and train branches where you want them by loosely winding stiff wire around them. Repot established plants every two years in spring in the same shallow container. Cut away a third of the roots and pull away the old compost. Liquid feed every six weeks.
problems they aren't easy and hate draughts and radiators.

Other peculiar plants *stag's horn fern (p153), cock on a plate (p38), the devil's backbone (p147)*

CLIMBERS + TRAILERS

Trailing plants are mostly just climbers without any support that are allowed to go floppy. They don't need much special care and if they get long and leggy, just chop back the stems to make them a bit tidier. Climbers, on the other hand, need training because they don't really do it on their own so you have to give them a helping hand. Wind new shoots in before they become too long and woody and, if necessary, tie branches in with a loop of green garden string. Don't tie it too tightly though or you'll garrotte the stems and chop the plant in half.

Climbers can be trained up anything including something permanent like banisters, shelves or vertical wires fixed to the wall. But if you're shoving a support into a pot, place it towards the outer edge so you don't damage any roots. Moss poles should probably be banned. Basically a bamboo cane with a load of moss wrapped around it, they are useful for holding up heavy plants like philodendron and cheese plants, and aerial roots can be poked into them, but they aren't pretty.

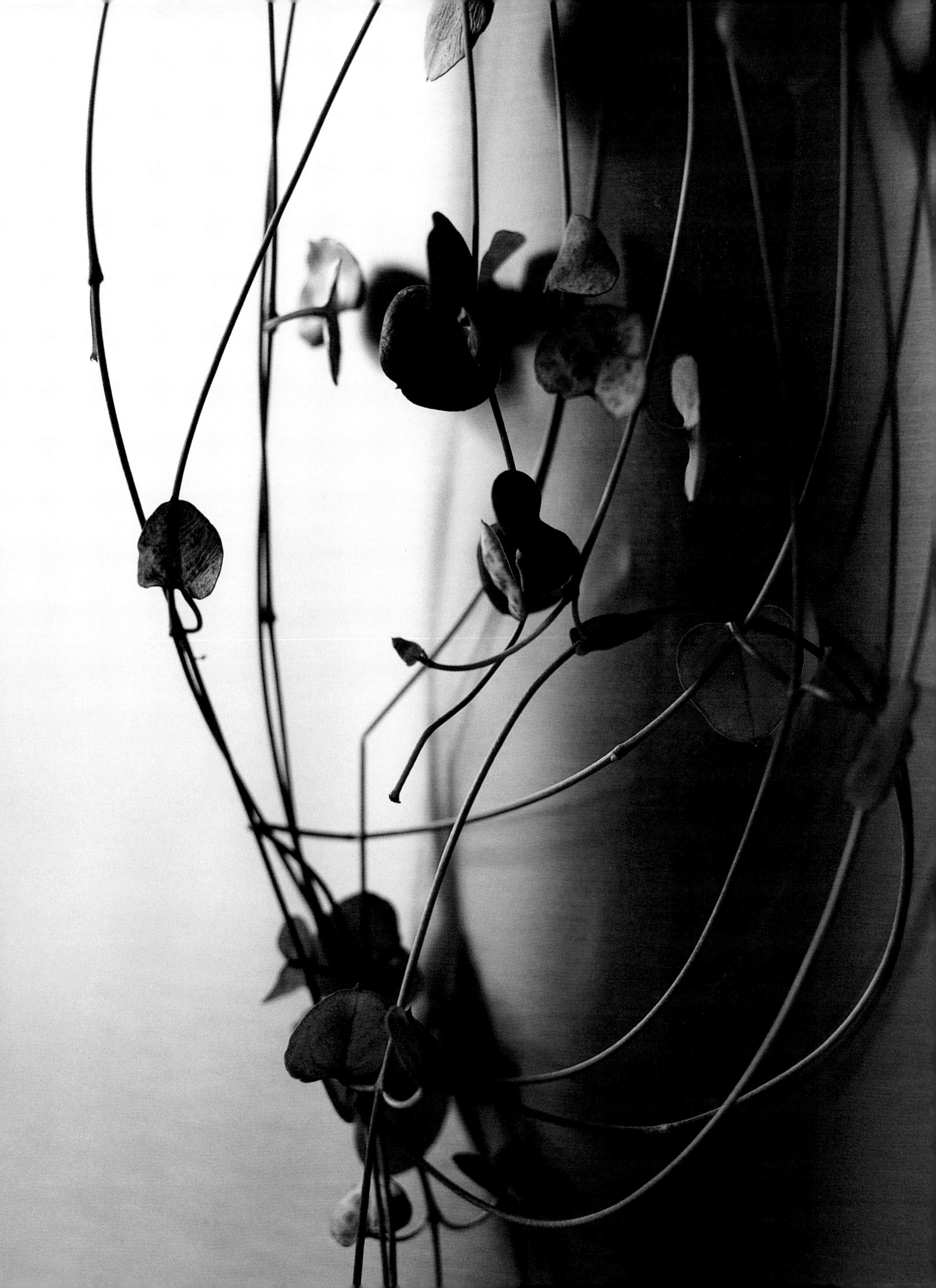

SWEETHEART PLANT (page 50)
Philodendron scandens

You can't really go wrong with this climbing or trailing plant which is perfectly happy in most homes. The pointy heart-shaped leaves are a bronzy colour at first and then turn deep green. Keep it bushy by pinching off the shoot tips every now and then.

light bright light is best but it will survive in darker corners.

temperature average warmth. It won't be happy below 13°C.

water moderately in spring and summer, enough to keep soil moist, and give a fortnightly liquid feed. In winter, let compost dry out a little.

special needs to propagate, take 7.5–10cm tip cuttings in late spring or early summer.

problems avoid direct sun. If it's too warm in winter it produces weedy leaves which must be cut off.

ROSARY VINE (page 51)
Ceropegia linearis woodii

This weird trailing succulent is very easy to grow. It produces thin dangling stems with fleshy dark green marbled leaves which are silvery white on top and purple beneath. From late summer to early autumn, happy plants will produce lots of dull pink tubular flowers.

light thrives in bright light.

temperature does well in any normal room temperatures but it will live down to 5°C.

water sparingly, it is best to allow top half of compost to dry out before next watering. Feed monthly in spring and summer.

special needs plant up tuberous growths which are produced along the stems.

problems if it's too wet in winter it will rot.

CREEPING FIG (below)
Ficus pumila

This pretty little thing is normally a trailing plant but if it's happy it will grow up a wall, sticking to it with aerial roots. The 2cm heart-shaped leaves are slightly puckered and there is also a variegated form (pictured). They look good grown at the base of other larger plants.

light bright light, avoid direct sun.

temperature flourishes in cooler temperatures, almost capable of withstanding frost. In centrally heated rooms, you must keep the humidity up.

water always keep moist and never allow roots to become dry or its leaves will shrivel.

special needs give a liquid feed fortnightly between spring and autumn.

problems red spider mite if the humidity is low.

CAPE LEADWORT (below)

Plumbago auriculata

This climber is normally trained over a hoop of wire when young. Wind in new shoots, but it's quite speedy so you'll then need to train it up something. It flowers from spring to autumn and comes in pale blue or occasionally white.

light loves full sunlight.

temperature cool to average, but in winter a cool rest at 8–10°C.

water loads during the active period, but don't stand in water. In winter give just enough to stop it drying out.

special needs feed fortnightly from spring to summer with a high-potash tomato-like fertilizer.

problems flowers are only produced on the current year's growth so trim the old stems back in spring to encourage new shoots and therefore flowers.

BLEEDING HEART VINE

Clerodendrum thomsoniae

An excellent 3–4m high climber for the conservatory, it can also be kept pruned as a pot plant for the house. The 12cm long leaves are corrugated and not particularly pretty but in spring, summer and early autumn there are clusters of white puffed-out flowers with scarlet tips.

light bright filtered light for flowers.

temperature average warmth. It will only flower if kept humid during active growth and given a cool winter rest.

water plentifully in active growth and sparingly in winter.

special needs liquid feed every two weeks except winter. In spring prune stems back by half and pinch out tips regularly if you want a small plant.

problems none in particular.

IVY

Hedera helix

There are loads of these green and variegated fast-growing small-leaved ivies. They have little aerial roots that cling onto anything so they're great climbers, yet they can also be left to trail or be trained round hoops of wire and regularly trimmed.

light bright or medium light.

temperature cool or even cold rooms. Raising the humidity is very important in warm, heated rooms.

water moderately and slightly less in winter. Don't let compost dry out.

special needs liquid feed every other week in active growth. Cut shoots back occasionally to keep it bushy and use them for cuttings.

problems Red spider mite is very common in warm rooms. Chuck the plant away rather than trying to cure bad infestations.

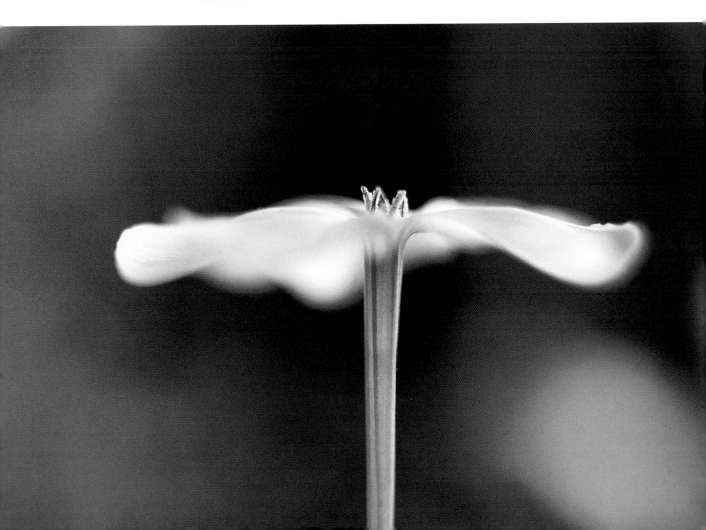

GRAPE IVY (above left)
Cissus rhombifolia

This is a tough old plant that is extremely tolerant of poor conditions. It can climb or trail and can grow at least 50cm a year. It will soon reach about 3m if it's got something to grow up. The leaves are silvery beneath and deep glossy green on top.

light ideally bright light, yet will tolerate anything but strong sun.

temperature average warmth but during the winter prefers a rest at a much cooler 13°C.

water moderately during the active period and feed fortnightly. In winter only keep the compost just moist.

special needs to propagate, take young tip cuttings, 7.5–15cm, long in spring.

problems strong sunlight will scorch the leaves and mildew is common especially if the compost is too soggy.

CHESTNUT VINE (above right)
Tetrastigma voinierianum

This is the mother of all vines with each leaf measuring more than 30cm in length once it's unfurled. The only drawback is that it's quite rampant, so you need loads of space to accommodate it. High ceilings or a tall conservatory is essential.

light needs bright light.

temperature average temperature, but not hot centrally heated rooms. They hate warm, dry air and dramatic fluctuations in temperature.

water moderately from spring to autumn, but ease off a bit in winter.

special needs feed fortnightly from spring to autumn. To propagate, take 25cm long tip cuttings any time except winter.

problems it grows so fast you'll have to prune it a lot.

PAPER FLOWER (right)
Bougainvillea glabra

Ubiquitous in the Mediterranean and the sub-tropical world, this climber will flower well in spring and summer of its first year, but it is difficult indoors. You need a conservatory for further flowering.

light the sunniest place you've got.

temperature average warmth, but in the winter months keep cool – down to about 10ºC.

water water moderately so it's just moist, but keep almost dry in winter. Feed fortnightly while in flower.

special needs stem cuttings in summer are quite easy.

problems too much heat in the winter months makes it suffer.

PASSION FLOWER
Passiflora

There are hundreds of different passion flowers, but not all are suitable for growing indoors. *P. citrina*, with yellow flowers, can be kept as a small vine less than a metre high and it can flower all year except the winter months. *P. sanguinolenta* has pinky red flowers, *P.* x *allardii*, the purple-flowered *P.* 'Amethyst' and the red-fruited *P. rubra* are all scented. The one drawback is that flowers only last for a day or two.

light lots of light, even a south-facing window.

temperature average but keep the humidity up. Spray leaves daily.

water moderately, although they are thirsty plants and in summer usually need daily watering.

special needs when they get overgrown, unravel and prune out as much as half the shoots to within 15cm of the main branches. Feed regularly while in active growth.

problems red spider mite.

Other climbers and trailers
philodendron (p19/21), devil's ivy (p44), wax flower (p87), jasmine (p84)

55

COCONUT PALM

BIG

Big is beautiful and some species only look good once they reach stately proportions. Because most plants grow quite slowly indoors, it's worth investing a bit of cash in something magnificent. Large plants should be treated as pieces of furniture or artworks and incorporated into room designs rather than stuck in as an afterthought. So don't just go out and buy a huge palm and then figure out where to put it when you get home. Big plants can be quite pricey so, to protect your investment, make sure you choose the right plant for the right place and give it some space so it doesn't get bashed into and damaged.

BIG

COCONUT PALM (page 56)
Cocos nucifera

This is probably the best value-for-money plant there is. The nursery just shoves a coconut in a pot, it sends up a few 1.5m leaves and then they sell it. You can expect to keep it looking good for a couple of years and then it should really be binned.

light bright filtered light near a window is best.

temperature average warmth.

water moderately all year but it doesn't seem to mind neglect.

special needs put it into a bigger pot so it doesn't topple over and a fortnightly feed won't go amiss.

problems none really.

TUFTED-FISHTAIL PALM
Caryota mitis (page 57)

These unusual palms are slow growing, but they will reach a couple of metres high and develop a spreading crown. Small plants look rubbish so pick a big one. Lots of light is the key to success.

light bright or filtered light.

temperature average. The warmer it is, the more humidity is needed.

water plenty of water in summer, but go easy in the winter just enough to stop the soil drying out.

special needs feed every other week except winter.

problems red spider mite can be a problem. Lower fronds naturally go yellow and drop off.

BANANA PLANT (below)
Musa acuminata 'Dwarf Cavendish'

Bananas grow really fast, about a metre a year, with plenty of warmth, water, food and light. The leaves are easily damaged so wrap it up well before you take it home.

light bright with some direct sun.

temperature average warmth, but give it good humidity.

water needs plenty in the active period, add liquid feed every time. In winter water sparingly.

special needs propagate in the spring by removing suckers and planting up.

problems watch out for red spider mite under the leaves.

DRACAENA (above left)
Dracaena deremensis 'Warneckii'
Dracaenas have long, strap-shaped, often, stripy leaves. They are mostly erect plants that develop a single cane or trunk as the lower leaves fall off with age. All are pretty easy to keep and basically have the same requirements. This particular variety has white and green stripy leaves and reaches about 1.8m high.

light bright but not direct sunlight.

temperature average warmth protected from draughts. They don't like the cold at all.

water plentifully so the compost is always moist but never ever soggy. Water sparingly in winter. Feed every other week in active growth.

special needs repot every two years using a soil-based compost because it is heavier and stops tall plants from falling over.

problems overwatering is a big killer. Dry air or soil makes leaf tips go brown.

CANARY DATE PALM (above)
Phoenix canariensis
This classic palm tree will do well indoors if it gets plenty of light. The fronds are quite stiff so give it lots of space to make sure it won't poke people's eyes out. It is quite slow growing but it will eventually get to about 2m tall. The miniature date palm *P. roebelenii* is less than a metre high with more feathery, wide-spreading fronds and is an excellent air purifier.

light direct sunlight although *P. roebelenii* prefers bright filtered light.

temperature average warmth, but a cool winter rest as low as 10°C is best.

water plentifully in the growing period, but sparingly in winter, so the compost is barely moist.

special needs feed once every two weeks from spring to summer.

problems keep out of cold draughts. Yellowing fronds may be a result of irregular watering and low light.

BUDDHIST PINE
Podocarpus macrophyllus
Unheated rooms are really best for this conifer, cold hallways and porches are ideal. As it gets older, the branches start to droop and it becomes a fairly graceful little tree. They can reach several metres indoors if the pot is big enough. The tough flat green leaves are about 8cm long and not easily damaged.

light bright filtered light.

temperature cool to average warmth is best.

water moderately but allow to become fairly dry in winter unless in a warm room.

special needs some form of staking might be required. If a plant gets too open, trim back side shoots in spring to make it bushier. Repot each spring with a soil-based compost.

problems fairly trouble-free.

BIG

PONY TAIL PALM (left)
Beaucarnea recurvata
This is a really easy plant to grow. The plume of grassy leaves give the plant its common name but it's also called elephant's foot because of the swollen base of the usually single grey stem. Fairly slow growing, it's a good idea to buy big.
light bright with a little sun.
temperature average warmth, dry air isn't a problem.
water give it a good soak, then leave it until it becomes moderately dry. Avoid overwatering.
special needs repot every other year in spring.
problems for some reason cats like chewing the leaves which doesn't seem to harm the cats but it doesn't do a lot for the plants.

UMBRELLA TREE
Schefflera actinophylla
This stately tree-like plant can reach a couple of metres high. There are between five and seven tough shiny leaves that radiate out from a central point like the spokes of an umbrella. They are quite easy plants to grow and are excellent air purifiers.
light bright light.
temperature ideally a cool room between 15–18°C, but they'll survive higher if the humidity is kept up. If it falls to below about 13°C, then leaves will drop.
water moderately in active growth but keep on the dry side in winter.
special needs feed every two weeks in active growth. Repot every other spring – small pots keep the plants small. Clean the leaves regularly with a sponge.
problems mealy bug and scale.

FIG (right)
Ficus 'Audrey'
Most of the different figs are pretty tough plants that are happy in most indoor environments. This one is similar in habit to the more common fiddle leaf fig, *Ficus lyrata*. Like the closely related rubber plant, *F. elastica* they grow very upright and very quickly, 30 or 40cm a year is normal.
light anywhere between medium and bright. Avoid direct sun.
temperature average warmth. Raising the humidity is only necessary in very warm rooms.
water sparingly so the compost is barely moist.
special needs sponge the leaves to remove dust.
problems overwatering makes the lower leaves drop.

NORFOLK ISLAND PINE
Araucaria heterophylla
This turns into a proper tree in a big conservatory, but is a bit more manageable indoors growing about 10–15cm a year. A feathery conifer, it has bright green needles on branches arranged in tiers.
light medium to bright light. If it's too dark the needles drop.
temperature they'll be happy in a really wide range from cool to warm but increase the humidity at the upper end.
water plentifully in active growth but only moderately in winter.
special needs repot every two years with a soil-based compost. Liquid feed every two weeks.
problems excessive central heating can make the needles crispy and eventually kills the plant. Keep away from radiators.

Other big plants *kentia palm (p68), rubber plant (p42), weeping fig (p71), philodendron (p63/65)*

OFFICE

Plants in offices are said to reduce absenteeism and improve worker output but they need to be fairly tough and low maintenance in order to thrive. In foyers, they must be able to survive draughts and perhaps an accumulation of cigarette butts in the pot. Elsewhere they need to have rugged leaves that won't get damaged by people brushing past them. They need to be able to put up with a fairly dry air-conditioned atmosphere and the occasional cup of coffee being chucked on their roots. On the plus side, most offices have fairly constant temperatures and the only problems are likely to arise if the offices get too cold at night when no one is there.

NARROW-LEAVED FIG (left)
Ficus barteri 'Variegata'
This is that little bit more resilient than the popular weeping fig *F. benjamina* and is less prone to shedding its leaves.
light bright, but not as much for the non-variegated sort.
temperature average warmth.
water moderately, allow compost to dry out a bit between waterings. Too much water makes the lower leaves fall.
special needs feed fortnightly in active growth, wash dust off leaves.
problems the milky white sap can be an irritant so don't get it in your eyes. Watch out for scale and mealy bug. Avoid radiators and draughts.

CORN PALM (page 62)
Dracaena fragrans 'Massangeana'
This is a particularly rugged plant and is good for removing toxins from the air. It can reach between 2–3m high. The closely related *D. deremensis* is just as good.
light prefers bright light but also grows in dimmer conditions.
temperature average warmth.
water keep moist, reduce in winter.
special needs repot every two years and feed every fortnight during active growth.
problems fairly trouble-free.

ARECA PALM
Chrysalidocarpus lutescens/ Dypsis lutescens
A feathery palm several metres high with lots of yellow stems. It does well near office windows, shaded by blinds or tinted glass.
light bright filtered light.
temperature average warmth. They don't seem to mind minor fluctuations and put up with low humidity better than kentias.
water somewhere between plentifully and moderately.
special needs liquid feed every two weeks in active growth.
problems draughts can make leaves dull greeny brown.

PHILODENDRON (page 63)
Philodendron
There are loads of philodendrons and they are all good in offices. There are some, like *P. selloum* and *P. bipinnatifdum,* with rosettes of massive leaves which need a lot of space and then there are the climbing sorts like *P. scandens* (p50/52) and the one pictured.
light bright filtered light. They'll survive dimmer conditions but plants get leggy.
temperature average warmth.
water moderately and then sparingly in winter.
special needs climbers need a moss pole or something for support. Poke the stubby aerial roots into the moss.
problems overwatering causes yellowing leaves. Leaves can be damaged by excessive battering.

ASPARAGUS FERN (right)
Asparagus setaceus
Not really a fern at all. It starts off bushy with its almost horizontal, almost triangular fronds but then turns into a twining climber sending out long winding shoots. These can be allowed to trail or be chopped off. *A. densiflorus* 'Sprengeri' is even tougher with drooping stems covered in needle-like leaves.
light bright light is essential, but not direct sunlight.
temperature average warmth.
water plentifully to keep it moist but sparingly in winter.
special needs liquid feed every two weeks during active growth. Repot in spring.
problems underwatering and low humidity can cause yellowing and dropping foliage. Pale leaves may also be due to red spider mite. Beware the tiny thorns on the stems.

JAPANESE ARALIA
Fatsia japonica
This green glossy leaved plant can be grown like the Ivy tree (page 20).

ADONIDIA PALM
Veitchia merrillii
This palm from the Philippines has a bright green trunk, swollen at the base. The chunky fronds are strongly arched. Reaching as much as 5–6m, this is a plant for foyers and large spaces. The Alexander palm, *Ptychosperma elegans*, is similar but often grown as a clump.
light bright, filtered light.
temperature average, above 15ºC.
water moderately, less in winter.
special needs liquid feed every fortnight in growth. Yellowing of fronds may be magnesium deficiency, apply liquid seaweed.
problems red spider mite, mealy bug.

Other office plants grape ivy (p54), kentia (p68), peace lily (p18/21), painted drop-tongue (p20)

SPINELESS YUCCA

UNKILLABLE

UNKILLABLE

Some people just can't keep plants alive no matter how hard they try. Others don't have the time or simply can't be bothered. But whether you've got green fingers or not, the simplest solution is to choose plants that refuse to die. There's nothing worse than a suffering plant that sits in the corner looking sad. So pick something indestructible that thrives on neglect, puts up with draughts or darkness, massive leaps in temperature and no affection whatsoever. Of course, nothing is totally indestructible; if you deprive anything of light or water it will eventually die, the only difference is that some die much faster than others. Cacti and succulents are classic examples – they only thrive if you give them lots of sunlight, water and fertilizer, but they'll cling onto life for ages without much of anything. The biggest killer of indoor plants is overwatering, so it's always safest to be stingy with it, but the plants here will mostly put up with extremely erratic watering by hopeless gardeners.

KENTIA PALM
Howea forsteriana
Probably the most popular indoor palm because it's so tough. It's actually several plants in one pot so it never forms a proper trunk.
light bright or medium light is fine. It can be kept in darker corners as long as you move it near to a window every other day.
temperature average. Low humidity isn't really a problem but very dry air makes leaf tips brown.
water plentifully but never stand in water. In darker cooler conditions water sparingly.
special needs small pots are fine, but repot every two or three years.
problems pale leaves and fine webbing underneath is caused by red spider mite.

SPINELESS YUCCA (page 66)
Yucca elephantipes
These familiar plants have a knobbly brown trunk with two or three clumps of green leaves at the top. As these clumps grow they also develop canes as the lower leaves fall off.
light bright light, if they don't get enough they will stop growing but still survive. Too much sun bleaches and scorches the leaves.
temperature average warmth but they'll survive down to 10°C.
water plentifully, keep the compost moist but much drier in winter. Fairly long periods without water don't cause much damage.
special needs if they get too tall chop through the cane and new shoots will appear just below the cut. Use the cane for cuttings.
problems trouble-free.

WANDERING JEW
Tradescantia zebrina/Zebrina pendula
This almost trailing plant has iridescent oval leaves about 5cm long with two broad silver stripes. Underneath they are purple. In spring and summer it produces small purple, three-petalled flowers. Other cream and green (and sometimes pink) tradescantias are very similar but trail a bit more.
light bright light is best. They'll survive in less but get leggy and the leaf colour fades a bit.
temperature cool or average warmth. The warmer it is the faster they grow.
water moderately in active growth and sparingly in winter. They don't seem to mind a bit of neglect.
special needs If they get leggy chop them back. The cuttings root easily in compost or in a glass of water. Put at least five in a pot. Regularly pinch out shoot tips to keep compact.
problems none really, apart from getting leggy.

MADAGASCAR DRAGON TREE
Dracaena marginata (page 67)
This plant actually improves with neglect. The narrow green leaves with red edges are gradually replaced by thinner, prettier leaves if deprived of bright light and the stems grow a bit crooked.
light likes bright light but is happy well away from windows.
temperature average warmth.
water moderately in the growing season, but go easy in winter. Doesn't mind underwatering, but too little can cause brown leaf tips.
special needs feed occasionally.
problems none really.

MOTHER-IN-LAW'S TONGUE (right)
Sansevieria trifasciata 'Laurentii'
This succulent was once incredibly popular and has since been out of favour but it's set for a comeback. Perhaps its greatest asset is its unkillability for which it scores 9.5.
light bright light but can also withstand direct sunlight.
temperature average warmth but won't grow in cold rooms.
water moderately but keep fairly dry in winter.
special needs propagate by leaf cuttings. Feeding isn't important.
problems overwatering makes the base of the stems rot and leaves go yellow.

SPIDER PLANT
Chlorophytum comosum 'Vittatum'
Barely a toilet in the land has eluded the humble spider plant. Cascading stems with small white flowers turn into tiny plantlets – miniature imitations of the green-and-white striped parent.
light really adaptable. Anything except extreme sun or shade.
temperature warm or fairly cold rooms. Doesn't mind dry air.
water plentifully in the active period, moderately in winter.
special needs feed fortnightly, but it isn't essential.
problems excess heat or dark makes leaves pale and limp.

UMBRELLA PLANT
Schefflera arboricola
Also called *Heptapleurum arboricola* this is a smaller relative of *S. actinophylla* (p60). Very hard to kill, it will reach nearly 2m in ordinary room conditions and keeps growing almost year round. Each leaf is made up of about ten leaflets each on a stalk like the spokes of an umbrella. There is a fairly garish variegated form.
light bright, but medium is ok.
temperature average warmth.
water moderately but will cope with a bit of forgetfulness.
special needs pinch out the growing tips to encourage branching otherwise they just keep going straight up and eventually topple over. They seem to grow happily in a tiny pot but repotting each year is preferred. Liquid feed every few weeks in active growth.
problems sudden changes or hot dry air can cause a bit of leaf drop but they won't die.

Fire

WEEPING FIG (left)
Ficus benjamina
Probably the best indoor plant in the world. It only manages to get in here by a nose on account of its penchant for dropping all its leaves. But even if that does happen, it won't die and they'll grow back. There are lots of different varieties around these days and the various variegated ones are good but need a little more light.
light bright light is best.
temperature average warmth but it acclimatizes well to most rooms.
water moderately. Erratic watering isn't too much of a problem. Liquid feed fortnightly in active growth.
special needs moving the plant around and sudden changes in conditions can make the leaves drop but new ones grow back.
problems scale insects, and overwatering will cause lower leaves to fall.

FLAMING KATY (below left)
Kalanchoe blossfeldiana
You can't actually kill this flowering succulent, even if you try. They flower for months and months but once they've finished they are best chucked away. They grow to between 15 and 20cm high and flower in red, pink and yellow.
light a sunny window-sill is ideal.
temperature average warmth but is happy in colder rooms.
water it doesn't need much water so keep it on the dry side.
special needs feed every two weeks while in flower, but it isn't essential. Remove the flowers when they fade if you can be bothered.
problems none really.

CAST IRON PLANT (below right)
Aspidistra elatior 'Milky Way'
The Victorians named this plant because it put up with their gas-light rooms and coal-fire fumes. It seems to do best if you don't do anything to it. Grown for its leaves, it does also produce inconspicuous little purple flowers at ground level.
light will survive in dark corners but prefers medium light. Variegated ones need medium to bright light.
temperature very adaptable.
water moderately and not very often. Allow top two-thirds of the compost to dry out between waterings. Liquid feed every two weeks in the growing period.
special needs aspidistras do best when they are left alone. Repot only if it needs it after three or four years.
problems generally trouble-free but watch out for red spider mite.

Other unkillable plants
ivy (p53), ivy tree (p20), philodendron (p19/21), peace lily (p18/21), parlour palm (p21)

CHALLENGING

If you think about it, plants aren't meant to be grown indoors anyway and quite frankly it's a miracle that so many different ones will do so well in your living room. Sadly, it's human nature for us to want things that we can't have and people try to grow plants that just don't want to be inside and yearn for the great outdoors, or at the very least a conservatory. But for anyone who likes a challenge, here are a few plants that are worth a bit of extra hassle.

JUNGLE FLAME (below left)

Ixora coccinea

They won't put up with much deviation from their ideal growing conditions. This evergreen shrub, with glossy green leaves, flowers when it's very small but it can get to over a metre high. There are varieties with orange, yellow, pink and red flowers which appear in summer.

light bright light on a window-sill is best.

temperature average warmth with high humidity.

water moderately and then sparingly after flowering.

special needs liquid feed every two weeks in spring and summer. Repot each spring but just topdress older plants.

problems scale insects can appear and all the leaves fall off if you don't get the watering right.

ROSE GRAPE (below right)

Medinilla magnifica

A warm greenhouse or conservatory only makes it slightly easier to grow this tricky customer. They can reach a metre tall and, in late spring, the pink flower heads extend to 45cm long. To have any hope of getting them to flower, however, you must pamper them continually.

light bright filtered light is essential for this plant.

temperature they must be kept constantly warm, between 20 and 26°C, with a consistently high humidity. A winter rest at about 18°C is needed.

water moderately with a fortnightly liquid feed in spring and summer. Water sparingly in winter.

special needs immediately after flowering in early summer cut all branches back by half.

problems red spider mite loves it.

DUTCHMAN'S PIPE (page 72)

Aristolochia gigantea

A warm conservatory or greenhouse is really needed for this evergreen twining climber which can reach 10m but, in theory, it could be grown in a large, warm, bright room. In summer it has bizarre chocolate-purple flowers, sometimes the size of a head. Flowers are borne on old stems.

light bright filtered light.

temperature average warmth.

water freely and apply liquid feed monthly from spring to autumn. In the winter months, water sparingly.

special needs softwood cuttings in early spring. Prune after flowering.

problems mostly trouble-free, but can get rampant so needs plenty of space.

MAIDENHAIR FERN (page 73)
Adiantum raddianum
This beautiful feathery fern has black wiry stems and delicate pale green fronds. Sadly, they are so delicate that a little too much heat or a missed dose of water and the fronds shrivel and die. Brightly lit bathrooms seem to be the best place for them. They also love bottle gardens.
light bright sunlight, never full sun.
temperature very cool conditions. Raise the humidity in warm rooms. Cold rooms aren't a big problem.
water keep the compost always just moist but never soggy. Never let it dry out. Give a monthly liquid feed at half strength except in winter.
special needs trim off damaged or dead fronds. Repot occasionally in spring.
problems hates fluctuations in temperature.

BIRD OF PARADISE
Strelitzia reginae
Keeping them alive is easy but getting them to flower in ordinary room conditions is nigh on impossible unless you move them around. You really need a conservatory. Normally growing to around a metre high, the paddle-shaped leaves are on the end of long stalks with orange and blue flowers in late spring and early summer. Plants only flower when about six years old.
light bright light with a little direct sun (although not at midday) is essential for flowering.
temperature average warmth while in active growth but in winter, a cool, possibly unheated room at about 13°C. Without this rest, they won't flower.
water moderately in active growth and sparingly in winter.
special needs liquid feed every two weeks in active growth. Repot in spring.
problems scale insect on the undersides of the leaves.

AFRICAN HEMP (right)
Sparmannia africana
This large-leaved plant can reach several metres tall and it isn't hard to keep alive. But it is difficult to get it to flower and then keep it flowering. The double-flowered 'Flore Pleno' and the basic species are notoriously hard to coax into bloom so if you can, get the dwarf form 'Nana' and treat it as best you can.
light bright filtered light.
temperature constant cool temperatures of about 15°C.
water moderately and give a fortnightly liquid feed from spring. In the winter water sparingly.
special needs remove the flowers once they've finished because on their own, they won't fall for ages.
problems whitefly and red spider mite are very common in normal room conditions.

FIRECRACKER FLOWER
Crossandra infundibuliformis
It's hard enough to pronounce its name let alone keep it alive. Growing to about 60cm tall with glossy green leaves, in spring and summer they produce orangey-red tubular flowers, flared at the ends. Even very young plants flower. The problem is they absolutely must have a very high humidity which is difficult in your living room.
light bright light but no direct sun.
temperature average warmth. They don't like the cold.
water moderately so the compost is always moist. In winter, sparingly.
special needs keep that humidity up. Slotting it amongst other plants helps, daily misting and a pebble tray are essential.
problems red spider mite is common.

Other challenging plants *some orchids (p137–139), jewel plant (p78), gardenia (p82/84), wax flower (p87)*

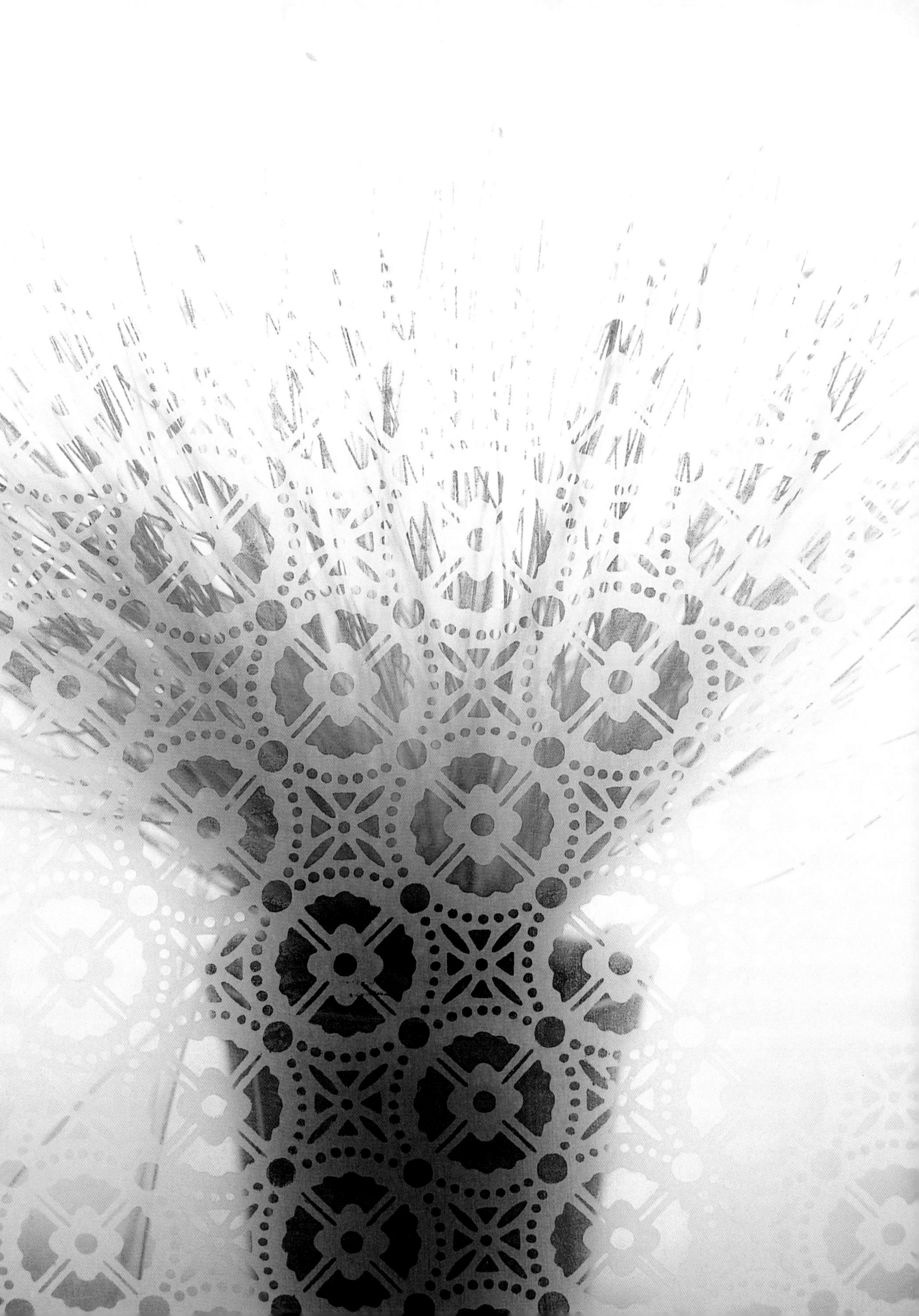

DAMP

Most indoor plants are killed because their owners give them too much water. So it's nice to have a few plants that like to get their feet wet and won't suffer a soggy end. Some like to be permanently moist but not waterlogged. Others can even be stood in a saucer or other container of water during the growing season. One advantage is that you can go off on holiday and not have to worry. The deeper the saucer, the longer you can go away for. You also don't have to fuss about accurate watering techniques because you can see when you've given it enough.

KRIS PLANT (above left)
Alocasia x amazonica
This amazingly beautiful waxy
leaved plant is unfortunately a bit
tricky to grow as an indoor plant
as it likes to be very warm and
humid. It's better off in a
conservatory but as it's so striking
give it a go anyway. Smaller plants
are best for indoors.
light bright light, but away from
direct sun.
temperature likes it warm,
at least 20°C. Avoid cool rooms.
Humidity must be permanently
high. Keep away from radiators.
water keep compost permanently
wet but only just moist in winter.
problems temperature
fluctuations, cold and draughts
can cause yellowing and spotted
leaves. Watch out for mealy bugs.
Contact with sap may cause
skin irritation.

FAIRY MOSS (above right)
Azolla filiculoides
This is a pond plant really but the
tiny delicate fronds look pretty
good floating around in a bowl on
the window-sill or a centrepiece
for a table. It keeps the water clear
on its own.
light give it bright light.
temperature puts up with a
whole range of conditions.
water grow in a bowl of water
and never let it dry out.
special needs even a tiny piece of
plant will quickly spread to cover
the whole surface of a bowl, so
propagating is easy.
problems ducks like eating it, but
that shouldn't be too much of a
problem in your kitchen.

JEWEL PLANT
Bertolonia marmorata
This is a tricky plant to look after
in the home and consequently not
very common. High humidity is
essential. They form a low clump
of shimmering dark green heart-
shaped leaves about 15cm long
with five silvery lines running
lengthways. Small purple flowers
occasionally appear.
light bright or medium light.
temperature warm rooms but
with a high humidity.
water plentifully during active
growth but only sparingly in winter.
special needs be careful not to
get water on the leaves which can
cause brown marks.
problems lack of humidity
encourages red spider mite and
brown-edged leaves.

DAMP

MIND YOUR OWN BUSINESS
Soleirolia soleirolii
A perfect common name for this creeping plant that spreads everywhere. Even in the confines of a pot it will sort of pour over the sides. It has tiny green leaves and doesn't flower. It's very good for growing at the base of large plants. There is a silvery variegated form and a golden yellow one.
light bright or medium, but it is adaptable. It will get straggly if it's too dark and tends to grow towards the light so rotate pots weekly.
temperature cold to average warmth, it can even live outside.
water plentifully from underneath, never let the compost dry out but don't stand plants in water.
special needs trim leggy plants with scissors. Liquid feed every four weeks. Easily propagated by pushing little bits into compost.
problems variegated plants sometimes turn green.

BULRUSH (page 76)
Scirpus cernuus
This graceful little plant looks like a clump of grass and has tiny whitish flowers on the tips of the bright green leaves. Small plants are upright at first and, as the leaves reach their full 25cm, they flop over but in a good way.
light medium or bright light, put them on a north-facing window-sill
temperature average warmth, but will be happy down to about 8°C in winter.
water stand in water unless kept at lower winter temperatures.
special needs liquid feed once every four weeks. Propagate by division, pull clumps apart in spring.
problems change water regularly, if stale water is left in the saucer, especially in cooler temperatures, it starts to stink.

CLUB MOSS (below + page 77)
Selaginella
These plants look like sort of ferny mosses. Some are only a few centimetres high while others get to a stately 30cm tall. They like the humidity of bathrooms and are at home in shallow pots of free-draining compost.
light they hate direct sun. Keep in medium light away from windows.
temperature average warmth but keep the humidity up. They aren't good with central heating and dry air is fatal.
water give it plenty, but don't ever let the pot stand in water.
special needs give them a trim in spring to neaten them up a bit if they need it. A weak liquid feed once a month is fine.
problems plants yellowing then turning black is due to bad watering. Make sure they aren't waterlogged and don't water the leaves.

DAMP

ARUM OR CALLA LILY (left)
Zantedeschia

The white-flowering type is quite common but now there are some smaller more colourful soft pink, yellow and carmine varieties. They flower in early summer and grow to about 40cm. In winter, the leaves die down.

light bright light with some direct sunlight.

temperature when it is starting into growth in the early spring months keep cool at a temperature of 10–13°C for about two months. Raise to average warmth when flowering.

water sparingly from early spring and as growth increases so should the water. Once in full leaf, stand the plant in a saucer of water. When the plant stops flowering reduce the water again and keep the compost fairly dry in winter. Liquid feed every two weeks in full leaf until flowering stops.

problems susceptible to fungal diseases and prone to aphids.

FLAME VIOLET
Episcia cupreata

In summer, red and yellow flowers are produced in groups of three or four on these low spreading plants. The leaves are a wonderful coppery green with silvery markings around the central vein.

light bright light with a bit of direct sun but not at midday.

temperature average warmth with essential high humidity.

water plentifully to keep compost constantly moist. In cooler temperatures ease off a bit. *E.* 'Cygnet' can be stood in water.

special needs liquid feed at a quarter strength every time you water it.

problems watch out for aphids on young leaves.

UMBRELLA PLANT (right)
Cyperus alternifolius

This easy rush has straight stems about a metre tall topped by a tuft of grassy leaflets. *Cyperus papyrus* is a magnificent, majestic plant of biblical fame, but much harder to grow. The pith of the stout 2m triangular stems has been used for making paper since ancient times. *C. involucratus* 'Gracilis' is a much shorter 30cm variety.

light grow in bright light.

temperature average warmth, but slightly cooler in winter. *C. papyrus* likes to be a bit warmer than the others all year.

water impossible to overwater, stand the pots in any watertight container and liquid feed every fortnight.

special needs crowded plants can be repotted in spring and divided at the same time to make more plants.

problems the water may start to smell so change it every now and then.

SWEET FLAG
Acorus gramineus 'Variegatus'

This grassy plant makes clumps of green and white striped leaves about 40cm tall. Quite a tough little plant, it doesn't mind cold, draughts or waterlogging.

light bright light.

temperature cool rooms are best, preferably unheated in winter.

water stand them in water; if they dry out the leaf tips go brown.

special needs propagate by dividing the plants at any time.

problems red spider mite can be troublesome in warm rooms.

Other damp plants *cock on a plate (p38), blechnum fern (p153), tufted-fishtail palm (p57/58), bleeding heart vine (p53)*

SCENTED

Smell is the most powerful and evocative of all the senses and is hugely important indoors when even the slightest perfume can fill a room. But it's a very subjective thing. What may smell fantastic to me may be revolting to you. Different times of day and different temperatures will also play their part, so what you'll find here are things that I think have a wonderful perfume but the best advice is try before you buy. Some of these plants are hard to coax into bloom for a subsequent year so they should all be bought in bud or in flower. That way, you're guaranteed to get your money's worth.

SCENTED GERANIUM (left)
Pelargonium

It's the leaves of geraniums that are scented. They can smell of lemon, peppermint, apple and all sorts of things. There are even some unpleasant ones that smell of fish and the London Underground. They are really easy to grow and can survive neglect.

light as much light as possible, direct sunlight would be great.

temperature average warmth. A cool winter rest is preferable in a cold room.

water thoroughly, then not again until compost looks dry. Keep almost dry in winter.

special needs pinch out tips in spring to keep plants bushy. Remove faded flower heads and yellow leaves. Stem cuttings in late summer are very easy.

problems excess water and humidity causes a black rot at the base.

JASMINE
Jasminum polyanthum

The pink-tinged, sweet-smelling flowers of this climber look good even in bud and it is more popular than the white- and yellow-flowered varieties because it flowers when it's quite young. If left to grow it will reach several metres high but it can be trained around a hoop of wire and kept to about 70cm high. The flowering period is mid-winter to mid-spring.

light bright, with some direct sun.

temperature cool conditions are best. They'll survive average warmth but won't flower as long.

water plentifully while it is in active growth.

special needs after flowering, cut plants back to keep them under control. Propagate by stem cuttings in spring and pinch out the tips of young plants.

problems warm rooms make plants struggle.

GARDENIA
Gardenia jasminoides (page 82)

Waxy white fragrant flowers appear in summer on this slow-growing bush. The mound of glossy green leaves usually gets to between 30–45cm high as an indoor plant. The smell is sweet and powerful. They are easy to keep but hard to get to flower.

light bright light, but never in direct sunlight.

temperature keep it at a steady 16–17°C with a high humidity when flower buds are forming. Once the buds have formed keep at average room temperature, up to a maximum of about 23–24°C, but keep it steady.

water moderately while in growth and very slightly less in winter.

special needs nip out long shoot tips in early spring to keep bushy. Feed every two weeks from spring to early autumn with azalea fertilizer.

problems sudden changes in temperature make buds drop off.

ANGELS TRUMPET (page 83)
Brugmansia/Datura

The curled buds unfurl into huge dangling 25cm long trumpet flowers. The most common are white, but yellow and orange are available. The scent, particularly in the evening, is overpowering to some. Ideally they are conservatory plants or can be put outside in the summer and kept somewhere cool indoors in winter.

light bright with some sun.

temperature average warmth but keep cool in the winter. An unheated room is best. They can be grown in a warm or cool conservatory.

water give it plenty from spring to autumn, sparingly in the winter.

special needs prune the plant almost to the ground in winter to save space. Feed every other week in spring and summer.

problems whitefly and red spider mite are common. All parts of the plant are poisonous.

STAR JASMINE
Trachelospermum jasminoides

An evergreen climber growing several metres tall indoors, it is really an outdoor plant (see Outside In, pages 166/169). From spring to summer, it has sweet-smelling jasmine-like flowers. The glossy leaves are green, but there is a prettier, less rampant variegated form.

light constant bright light, but shade from direct sunlight.

temperature always keep it cool.

water plenty in the growing season, just enough in the winter months to stop it drying out.

special needs liquid feed fortnightly from spring to autumn. Needs bamboo canes for support.

problems a bit of a rampant grower, but generally trouble-free.

CHERRY PIE

Heliotropium arborescens

This easy-to-grow plant has usually purple but sometimes blue or white flowers that do smell exactly like a cherry pie. It's uncanny. They flower in summer.

light lots of bright light, but avoid hot sun.

temperature average warmth but must be kept cool in winter.

water plentifully while active and sparingly in winter.

special needs liquid feed monthly in spring and summer. Prune in spring to keep it compact and remove dead flower heads. Propagate by stem cuttings in summer.

problems no real worries, but watch out for whitefly. Flowering deteriorates with age.

MINIATURE WAX PLANT (left)
Hoya lanceolata bella
These trailing plants are best in hanging baskets. They have pointy leaves and clusters of scented star-shaped flowers. The big brother, *Hoya carnosa*, is a fast-growing climber with bigger, glossy green leaves and similar waxy flowers. They thrive if left undisturbed apart from water and fertilizer.
light bright. A few hours of direct sun helps flowering of *H. carnosa*.
temperature average. *H. lanceolata bella* likes higher humidity.
water moderately from spring to autumn and then sparingly.
special needs only repot when it is unavoidable. Feed with tomato fertilizer every other week from spring to autumn.
problems sometimes mealy bug.

WAX FLOWER (below)
Stephanotis floribunda
This climber from Madagascar has clusters of pure white star-shaped tubular flowers that you get in bridal headdresses. It's tricky, but not impossible, to encourage back into flower in spring and early summer.
light bright light. Direct sunlight will damage the foliage.
temperature average warmth but hates sudden fluctuations. Keep the humidity up. In winter keep fairly cool.
water plentifully in summer and sparingly in winter.
special needs grow around a hoop of wire where space is limited. Liquid feed every two weeks in the active period. Repot in early spring.
problems scale insects under leaves and sometimes mealy bug.

PERSIAN VIOLET
Exacum affine
From midsummer to late autumn this little plant is covered in small, fragrant, violet-coloured flowers with a gold centre. Make sure you buy them mainly in bud rather than in bloom so you get the most out of them and then chuck them away when finished. They usually start off about 10cm tall and grow to about 25cm. There are also dwarf and white varieties available.
light bright light.
temperature cool or average warmth with high humidity.
water plentifully.
special needs liquid feed every two weeks. They can be grown from seed in late summer.
problems pick off blooms as they fade to prolong flowering.

Other scented plants *yesterday, today, tomorrow plant (p15), cereus (p142/143), peace lily (p18/21), hyacinth (p155/156), lily (p91)*

FENG SHUI

TI TREE (left) + POT CHRYSANTHEMUM (right)

Feng shui is about living in perfect balance with your environment, so every aspect of your life benefits. It's about channelling the flow of energy, and apparently growing the right plants in the right place makes a big difference. Succulents are the most auspicious, their plump, round leaves being symbolic of money and goodness, but thorny plants send out poisoned arrows of bad energy. Bonsai should be chucked out because they are intentionally stunted and are very bad for wealth and luck. But good feng shui can only be achieved if your plants thrive so look after them or the bad energy overwhelms the good chi. Oh and don't forget to put the toilet seat down or all your wealth will disappear into the sewer.

SILVER CROWN (left)
Cotyledon undulata
This succulent brings good fortune to your house and is quite easy to look after. It can be placed anywhere. The flowers are orange.
light full sunlight to avoid spindly growth and poor-coloured leaves.
temperature average warmth. Dry air is happily tolerated.
water moderately but reduce in winter, so compost almost dries out.
special needs liquid feed every two weeks during active growth.
problems none really.

TI TREE (page 88)
Dracaena or cordyline
Plants are appreciated for their shape and silhouette and, like bamboo, these plants are disciplined and upright. A number of species are sold like this. The canes are cut into sections and shipped overseas. Buds burst out the side at the top of the stem when stood in water or planted.
light medium light close to an east- or west-facing window.
temperature average warmth.
water moderately, keeping compost moist. Reduce in winter but don't let it dry out.
special needs liquid feed fortnightly in active growth.
problems leaves go soft and curly if temperatures are too low.

LILY
Lilium
Lilies represent good feng shui all year round. The big trumpet flowers are often scented and come in a range of colours including white, yellow and orange.
light bright light but not direct sun.
temperature cool rooms, especially at night while the bulb is getting ready to flower.
water plentifully while the bulb is growing.
special needs reduce watering after flowering. Put outside or in a cool room and repot in autumn.
problems rarely flower well again.

POT CHRYSANTHEMUM (page 89)
Chrysanthemum morifolium
Pure and honest, chrysanthemums are held in high esteem but yellow ones in particular are associated with a life of ease and they create great happiness and joy. Buy when the buds are showing colour because tight green ones may fail to open. Discard or plant in the garden after flowering.
light bright light is essential, but shade from midday sun.
temperature cool rooms are ideal. They'll survive average warmth if you increase humidity but won't flower for so long.
water plentifully before and during flowering. Don't let them dry out.
special needs feeding isn't necessary.
problems letting them stand in water has dire consequences.

GOLDEN-GROOVE BAMBOO
Phyllostachys aureosulcata
'Aureocaulis' (right)
Bamboo wards off malign spirits and symbolizes longevity and endurance. Have it on the left-hand side of your home to signify the dragon, at the front to attract good chi and at the back to be lucky in business. Old or dead growth must be removed immediately. Many bamboos suitable for indoors are quite tall and you may need a lot of space.
light needs permanently bright filtered light throughout the year.
temperature cool rooms are best for most species.
water plenty during the active period and during the winter only sparingly.
special needs feed every other week in active growth.
problems underwatering and excessive heat makes the leaves curl.

JADE PLANT
Crassula ovata
You've probably seen these tree-like plants in Chinese restaurants by the door to attract prosperity, but you can also put them in the kitchen for abundance. Don't let them get more than a metre high and if they get sick replace immediately. Fortunately these succulents are easy to look after.
light bright with some direct sun.
temperature cool or average.
water moderately while active, in winter enough so it doesn't dry out.
special needs liquid feed every two weeks, except in winter. Repot every two years. Propagate by leaf cuttings.
problems overwatering is a killer.

Other Feng shui plants orchids (p137–139), philodendron (p19/21), bulbs, especially daffodil, (p155–157), orange trees (p128–131), lady's eardrops (p32), many succulents (p144–149).

KEEPING

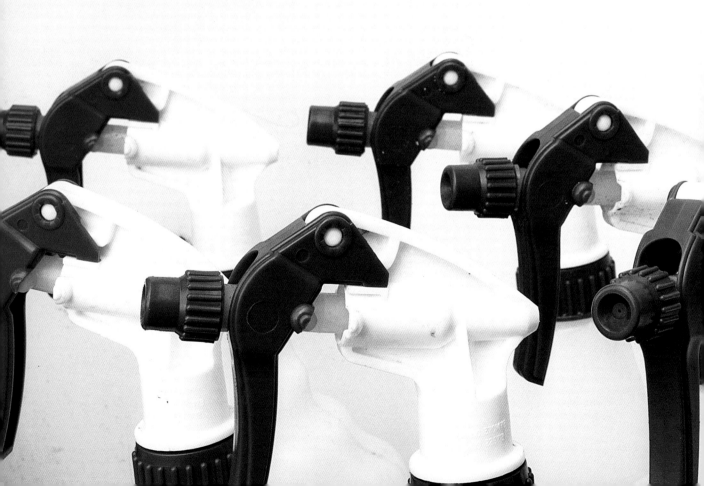

THEM HAPPY

LIGHT + ARTIFICIAL LIGHT

THE CHINESE ROSE, *Hibiscus rosa-sinensis*, needs to be by a window, but the extra sunshine makes plants more thirsty, so keep an eye on the watering.

Light is probably the most important factor that governs where you can keep a plant. As a general rule, flowering plants need to be near windows with lots of sunlight and foliage plants are happy in dimmer conditions. Always check each plant's individual requirements before deciding where to put it and, if in doubt, remember that too much light is far more damaging than too little.

Your eye is a surprisingly hopeless judge of light intensity, and as you move away from a window, the intensity drops dramatically. You can buy a simple light meter from a garden centre to measure whether one spot is significantly lighter or darker than another.

HOW MUCH LIGHT?

Always check a plant's light requirements first.

Full sun Close to a south-facing window where 100 per cent direct sunlight pours in for most of the day. Few plants can stomach this unless they're more than 60cm away from the window. Most cacti, succulents and pelargoniums are common exceptions.

Filtered sunlight Full sun as above, but the intensity is reduced by a tree outside the window or a translucent blind or sheer curtain. Or it may be an east- or west-facing window that gets plenty of sun, except at midday, when the sun is strongest.

Bright This suits the greatest number of plants. It's the area beyond full sunlight, at least 60cm back from a sunny window and extending about 1.5m into the room.

Medium A bit further still into a sunny room or close to a north-facing window. This type of light is the most common. Foliage plants will do fine but flowering plants won't do the business.

Dim Not many plants will thrive here. This is well into the room, perhaps 2.5m from windows where the light is poor, but you could just about read a newspaper during the day without artificial light. Plants in the medium light group can also live here for a few weeks or so before being moved back into more light.

TOO MUCH LIGHT

- Leaves scorched by the sun, brown or grey patches form.
- Whole leaves shrivel and die.
- Leaves are bleached by the sun and become washed out.
- Potting compost is baked dry.

NOT ENOUGH LIGHT

- New leaves are much smaller and pale.
- Plant doesn't appear to grow at all – if it does, growth is leggy.
- Lower leaves go yellow and drop.
- Variegated leaves turn green.
- Flowers are hopeless or don't even form.

HOW TO INCREASE LIGHT

- Paint your walls and ceilings white and hang lots of mirrors.
- Wipe dust from leaves so they can absorb more light.
- Hire a window cleaner.
- Move plants closer to the window in winter.
- Use artificial lighting.

ARTIFICIAL LIGHT

Longer days encourage stubborn plants like orchids and bromeliads to flower and others to flower for longer periods. Artificial lighting can supplement daylight and it's also pretty handy if you want to grow some sort of crop in a windowless room.

Spotlights/floodlights Ordinary indoor light fittings can only boost low light levels and can't be used as a substitute for daylight.

Fluorescent strip lights These can be used as a substitute for daylight. Especially good for seedlings, salads, herbs and small plants that need to be close to the light – between 30–60cm for foliage plants and even closer for flowering ones. The lights don't give off as much heat as ordinary bulbs, so won't scorch the leaves.

High Intensity Discharge lamps (HID) These hang-up and plug-in appliances are perfect for vegetables, flowers and other light-loving plants. The most efficient bulb is a 600W sodium bulb with a reflector. A 400W lamp uses less than 5 units per 12-hour day to run.

Reflection Surrounding plants with reflective material massively increases the available light. For crops it's worth fitting white lino or painting walls with white emulsion. Lining your loft with aluminium foil is not the answer, because it only reflects 55–70 per cent of light. Flat white paint or polystyrene sheets reflect 75–80 per cent and Mylar sheeting reflects 90 per cent.

Duration Most foliage plants will need between 12–14 hours of light a day and summer flowering plants between 16–18 hours.

WATER

Overwatering is the biggest killer of indoor plants. As soon as they show symptoms of distress the loving owner gives them even more water and they are literally killed with kindness. So if you're in any doubt – underwater.

WHEN?

Shove a finger into the potting compost as far as it will go. It should feel damp but not soggy. This is by far the best test – those clever electronic testers are just a waste of money. Most plants need frequent watering between mid spring and late autumn when they do most of their growing. It's after this that people cock it up – in most cases, you have to cut down on watering in winter because the plant won't use it. The compost gets waterlogged and the plants either die or produce ugly misshapen leaves.

HOW MUCH?

Flowering plants usually need more careful and regular watering than foliage plants, but check each plant in the relevant sections. They mostly fall into the following four categories.

Water sparingly Pour a splash of water onto the surface of the compost and let it seep in, but not so much that it comes out of the holes in the bottom of the pot. The aim is to just moisten the compost throughout, then let it nearly dry out between waterings.

Water moderately Most foliage plants fall into this one. Let the top centimetre or two of compost dry out between waterings. Then add a little water at a time, letting it soak in, and continue adding until a few drops appear at the bottom of the pot. The compost will then be moist throughout. You soon get the hang of the amounts with each individual plant. For plants that are watered from underneath, pour water into the saucer until it is no longer absorbed and the top layer of compost is moist. Pour away any water not soaked up.

Water plentifully This applies to most flowering plants. The compost wants to be moist (but not soggy) at all times, so must never dry out. Pour water onto the compost until it comes out the bottom of the pot, but don't actually leave it standing in water or the roots will rot. Any excess that remains by the time you've put your watering can away should be tipped out.

Standing in water No clues here. There are only a few plants in this category.

HOW?

A watering can is better than a jug or a glass because it pours the water right onto the compost and some hairy leaves can be damaged if you get water on them. So you don't slosh water all over the carpet, stick your finger over the end of the spout on your way back from the tap.

WHAT KIND OF WATER?

Tap water is usually fine, but best served at room temperature because cold water can shock the plant, slow down its growth and mark the leaves. Add a little water from the hot tap if in doubt.

But if you have hard water that makes your kettle fur up with lime, it can cause a few problems to certain plants. The best solution is to use rainwater or a simple water filter which will take out harmful chlorine and fluoride as well. Even easier still is to use the water out of a kettle that has previously boiled and cooled.

YOUR PLANT WILL NEED WATERING MORE FREQUENTLY THAN MOST IF . . .

- You've got the heating cranked up.
- Humidity in the room is low.
- It's in direct sunshine – especially in hot weather.
- It's a large plant in a small pot filled with roots.
- It has large, thin leaves.
- It's in active growth – usually summer but depends on the plant.
- It's flowering or fruiting.
- It's in a clay pot rather than a plastic one.

IF IN DOUBT, UNDERWATER. Although they don't like it, some foliage plants can cling onto life for weeks or even months without a drop.

PESTS, DISEASES + PROBLEMS

FINDING THE PROBLEM

Most indoor plants can be ravaged by different pests and diseases which can wreak havoc if untreated. Give plants a quick once over each time you water and treat anything suspicious immediately. Tell-tale signs are discoloured leaves and blotches. Bugs tend to hang out under the leaves or at the junction of leaves and stems so always check there first. If you can't see anything, the likely cause is incorrect watering, the wrong amount of light, heat or even draughts. If that still doesn't solve the problem you're probably better off chucking the plant away and getting a new one.

TREATMENTS

Organic cure Organic cures include picking bugs off by hand and squashing them between your fingers, but sometimes you have to resort to chemicals. As luck would have it there are some organic ones such as pyrethrum, but if you don't have anything to hand, you can dilute a bit of washing-up liquid and spray that on.

Biological controls Predators and parasites that you introduce to a plant to seek out and destroy a particular pest. They don't really like the environment of our homes, but work well in the controlled environment of conservatories and greenhouses where certain organic chemicals can be used simultaneously. Never use synthetic chemicals at the same time. The downside is that they usually need constant reintroducing and can't cope with bad infestations.

Chemicals If you're using synthetic chemicals, be aware that they're potentially dangerous, so you don't want to go spraying them about in the kitchen or all over your goldfish. In warm weather, you can take the plant outside, otherwise open all the windows. Better still, stick to one of the other solutions.

PREVENTION

Keeping plants healthy, well fed and watered is the best precaution, but pest and disease can still mysteriously appear as they are easily spread from one plant to another on air currents or by clothes as you brush past. Problems can hit at any time of year so being vigilant and taking immediate action are your best weapons. Inspect new plants and remove dead or damaged leaves.

APHIDS

This is an umbrella term for a bunch of roughly 2mm long, sap-sucking flies that come in black, pink, yellow or the popular green. They congregate on soft shoot tips and leaves, distort growth and you get the tell-tale honeydew and sooty mould, but they also spread plant viruses. They spread rapidly and moult regularly leaving behind empty 'skeletons'.

Organic cure Spray with pyrethrum, derris or insecticidal soap. Or rub off with fingers, but be careful on young shoots. You'll end up doing more damage than the aphids.

Biological control Parasitic wasp, *Encarsia formosa*.

Chemical Pirimicarb.

MEALY BUGS

Ugly squidgy ribbed insects, about 4mm long, that come in an unpleasant beige or pale pink. You can't miss them under leaves and on the leaf and stem junctions where they cover themselves in a sticky white cottony fluff. They also excrete honeydew.

Organic cure Wipe them off the plant with a damp cloth or a cotton bud or tiny paintbrush soaked in methylated spirit or spray the leaves with insecticidal soap.

Biological control A small, but unfortunately very ugly ladybird called *Cryptolaemus montrouzieri* is particularly useful when temperatures are higher in summer.

Chemical Remove by hand and spray with malathion.

WHITEFLY

Sap-feeding insects, about 2mm long, these live underneath the leaves and look like tiny white moths. When you tap the plant, the adults, which have white wings, all go totally ballistic. Whitefly can spread rapidly, excrete honeydew and also cause leaves to turn yellow and drop.

Organic cure Spray with insecticidal soap which doesn't harm the biological control, *Encarsia formosa*.

Biological Control Introduce *Encarsia formosa* between mid spring and mid autumn.

Chemical Spray with Permethrin a couple of times a week.

MILDEW looks like dusty grey patches on the leaf, which soon becomes yellow and blotchy.

PESTS, DISEASES + PROBLEMS

APHIDS (top left) MEALY BUG (top centre) WHITEFLY (top right)
RED SPIDER MITE (bottom left) SCALE INSECTS (bottom centre) BROWN LEAF TIPS (bottom right)

RED SPIDER MITE

One of the hardest pests to wipe out, these tiny sap-sucking insects which lurk beneath the leaves look like minute yellowish green spiders with two dark blotches. In the autumn they're a bit bigger and easier to spot and they also turn more orange. They can infest most indoor plants, especially those stressed out by hot, dry air. The first obvious sign is when the leaf develops a fine pale yellow or silvery mottling, so investigate the underside of the leaf. You've got to look really closely for the adults and the specks of whitish eggs. Another giveaway in extreme cases is a fine white webbing between stems and leaves. Raising humidity is the best deterrent and part of the cure.

Organic cure Spray with insecticidal soap, remove badly infected leaves and repeat treatments. Sacrifice a badly infected plant in order to save others.

Biological control *Phytoseiulus persimilis*.

Chemical Spray with malathion as soon as you find them. Repeat several times.

SCALE INSECTS

Like tiny limpets, these insects hide under a brown, waxy shell that they secrete over themselves. The young ones crawl about until they find a nice juicy stem or perhaps the main vein on a leaf and then they set up home. Scale insects are about 3–4mm in length and also excrete honeydew.

Organic cure Pick off by hand and wipe with insecticidal soap.

Biological control Parasitic wasp, *Metaphycus helvolus*.

Chemical Spray malathion on undersides of leaves every two weeks. Repeat three times.

BROWN LEAF TIPS

Brown leaf tips or edges, especially on long, narrow-leaved plants like dracaena, are usually caused by dry air or soil and sometimes by cold draughts. Another likely cause of this is too much fluoride in the tap water, so use filtered water, boiled water from the kettle that has cooled down or rainwater instead. The dead bits won't grow back. Either remove whole leaves, put up with the damage or buy a new plant.

MILDEW AND BOTRYTIS

Mildew (pictured on page 98) is a white, powdery fungal growth that appears initially on the surface of the leaf and then on other parts of the plant. Affected leaves go yellow, distorted and blotchy, look sick and usually drop off. Caused by dry soil and humid air around top growth, botrytis or grey mould is similar, but more furry and spreads all over the plant including the compost. Infected bits may go brown and soggy.

Organic cure Remove badly infected leaves and dust remaining leaves with sulphur. Improve ventilation.

Biological control None.

Chemical Spray with systemic fungicide or carbendazim. Cut out all botrytis-infected parts.

HONEYDEW

Sap-sucking insects latch onto the plant with their mouths and a sticky gunk pours out of their back ends. This splatters onto the leaf below (see bottom centre photograph) and under damp conditions, black patches of fungus called sooty mould grow on it. Unsightly rather than harmful, you can wipe it off with a damp cloth, but you need to sort out the pest that caused the problem in the first place.

OTHER COMMON AILMENTS

- **Wilting** Underwatering or overwatering, too much heat or pot-bound plants. Sudden collapse could be vine weevil that munch the edges of leaves at night. Wash off all compost and repot.
- **Leaf curl** Too cold, draughts or overwatering.
- **Sudden leaf drop** Shock caused by relocation of a plant (very common for weeping fig) or sudden change in temperature, light intensity, cold draughts or really dry roots.
- **Flower buds drop off or flowers fade fast** Underwatering, dry air, too dark.
- **Never flowers** Too dark or overfeeding.
- **Leaves pale and sad** Too much light.
- **Leaves go yellow and drop off** Overwatering or cold draughts or severe changes in conditions.
- **Brown patches on leaves** Scorchmarks caused by too much sunlight or physical damage.

TEMPERATURE + HUMIDITY

TEMPERATURE

The best plants as far as us humans are concerned are those which like a temperature range of about 18–24°C, because this is how warm we like to keep our houses. In The Plants you'll see this referred to as average warmth.

Many plants remain happy at lower temperatures, but anything higher than 24°C and you'll need to do something drastic to raise the humidity or the plants will snuff it.

At night time the temperature should ideally drop by about 3–6°C but if you get massive differences between day and night the plants won't like that either. Check the range with a max-min thermometer if you're worried.

THE RULES ARE

- Always pick the right plant for the right place or it'll suffer.
- Avoid danger spots like radiators, cookers and boilers.
- Bakingly hot window-sills with strong, direct sunlight pouring through a single pane of glass during the day will heat plants up too much.
- Avoid great fluctuations in temperature especially between day and night. Occasionally cranking the heating right up is bad news for plants.
- The space between a curtain and a window traps harmful cold air at night and excludes the benefits of the heated room.
- Leaves touching external window glass can get too cold, go black and die.
- Plants near external doors are subjected to draughts.
- Heat rising from a radiator can be good for some plants, but needs deflecting with a shelf and you'll probably have to raise the humidity as well.

DANGER SIGNS

- **Too cold** Leaves curl, go brown and drop off.
- **Too warm** Flowers die quickly and plants grow small leaves or weak leggy growth in good light. Lower leaves wilt and get brown crispy edges.
- **Sudden change in temperature and draughts** Rapid yellowing and leaf drop.

HUMIDITY

Humidity is the amount of water vapour held in the air, but it has nothing to do with how wet the compost is. A plant breathes through its leaves and as it does this it loses moisture by transpiration. If the humidity is very low, the plant will lose too much water and the leaves will dry up and shrivel. Thick leaves, like those of rubber plants, don't really suffer, but thin papery leaves like Angel's wings and some ferns will quickly die.

At low temperatures there isn't a problem, but as a room heats up the amount of water vapour in the air can't keep pace and it becomes dry. The main causes are central heating and rooms and conservatories with windows that get lots of direct sunshine.

HUMIDITY TOO LOW

- Leaf tips brown and shrivelled (especially spider plants, palms and dracaenas).
- Leaf edges turn yellow and may wilt.
- Buds fall and flowers wither.
- Leaves may drop off.

HUMIDITY TOO HIGH

- Patches of grey mould appear on leaves and flowers.
- Patches of rot on leaves and stem tips of cacti and succulents.

RAISING THE HUMIDITY

A pebble tray is the best solution. Fill a plant saucer with pebbles or gravel and top it up with water so the plant stands on the pebbles, but doesn't actually touch the water. As the water evaporates, it raises the humidity around the plant. The width of tray should be the same as spread of plant, but anything is better than nothing.

You can always put your plants in the bathroom as the humidity is normally higher in there. Just grouping plants together also helps and if you're really fussed you could buy a humidifier.

Misting your plants with one of those hand sprayer things is more or less a waste of time for a lot of plants because the effect is so short-lived. (However, it is essential for air plants – see Bromeliads, page 132). To lower humidity, improve ventilation.

KEEPING PLANTS NEXT TO A RADIATOR IS USUALLY A BAD IDEA. Leaves get scorched and they suck moisture out of the air.

POTTING + REPOTTING

WHY BOTHER?

A plant can stay in the same pot for years if you give it enough food and water, but eventually the roots will fill the pot and the compost will have disappeared. This is called 'pot-bound'. The plant will continually dry out, leaves will yellow and drop, so basically it means repot or die.

WHEN?

Younger plants may need repotting each year. The beginning of the active growing period (usually spring) is the best time because they'll recover from the shock more quickly. But don't repot sick or recovering plants – they're suffering already and it could all be a bit too much for them.

If roots are poking out the bottom of the pot, take it off and have a look. If you can hardly see any compost and all you're looking at is a dense mat of roots which are growing in a circle at the bottom of the pot, then you know it's time.

WHERE?

Give yourself a bit of space, the bath is good and the kitchen is always a safe bet, although neither tends to please other members of the household, especially if you start using the cutlery to prise things out of pots. If you venture outside to do it, make sure it's not a cold day or the plants will catch a chill. Equally if it's a sunny day, pick a place in the shade or the roots will get frazzled.

HOW?

- Water plants before you start.
- Clean previously used pots with soapy water and rinse.
- Move up one pot size at a time – an increase in diameter of about 2cm. Soak terracotta pots for about 15 minutes first.
- Put a layer of compost into the new pot and tap it sharply down on a hard surface to settle it. Stand the old pot in it to check the level isn't too high.

- Gently take off the old pot (if it's plastic you can cut it off with secateurs if necessary), snip off any damaged roots and pull off any old crocks. Check for bugs and grubs (see pages 98–101).
- Place the plant in the centre of the new pot and pour compost down the sides. Settle it gently with your fingertips but don't squash it in.
- Tap the plant down again a few times, top up the compost and water. The top of the root ball should be about 2cm below the rim of the pot to allow space for watering.

COMPOST

Ready-mixed indoor plant composts are the easiest. They usually contain nutrients that will feed the plants for about three months before you have to provide additional fertilizer. Peat-free potting composts are the alternative for the environmentally minded. Soil from the garden contains too many nasties and shouldn't be used.

TOPDRESSING

Eventually, plants sort of become adults and they reach an ultimate pot size. Instead of repotting, scrape off the top few centimetres of compost with a spoon or trowel, but be careful not to damage any major roots. Replace it with fresh compost mixed with a little slow-release fertilizer (see Feeding, page 108). Do this once a year and your plants will look far more perky.

CONTAINERS AND DRAINAGE

Any kind of container be used, but drainage is extremely important. If there aren't any drainage holes, either drill some or put a 5cm layer of gravel in the bottom. Excess water will sit here rather than rotting the roots and a crushed lump of barbecue charcoal in with the gravel will keep the water sweet.

Terracotta pots need crocks – fragments of broken pots or lumps of polystyrene – in their base to stop drainage holes getting bunged up. Plastic pots already have plenty of drainage holes.

If things are getting a bit crowded in the root department and you can barely see any compost, it's time to repot. This **GRAPE HYACINTH** isn't ready yet.

HYDROPONICS

Virtually any pot plants, whether ornamental or crop, can be grown by this soil-less culture which replaces the compost with an inert growing medium and a solution of nutrients dissolved in water.

ADVANTAGES OVER COMPOST
- Produces a more vigorous plant or crop in a shorter time.
- Watering and feeding are very simple and give exactly the required amount of nutrient to a plant.
- Saves time and space and is less messy.
- Soil-borne pests and fungi are avoided.
- For passive systems repotting is not done annually but only when a plant looks awkwardly too big for its container.
- Holidays aren't a problem with passive systems as feeding need only be done once every few months.

PASSIVE CULTURE
You can buy special double pots for this simplest form of hydroponics. The inner pot with holes in contains the plant and growing medium, which acts as an anchor for the roots, and the whole lot is suspended inside a watertight pot. The bottom of the inner pot is immersed in a nutrient solution which is sucked up by capillary action to reach the plant's roots. It's this combination of constant moisture, constantly available nutrients and high levels of air supply that make up the perfect root zone which the plants love. A special gauge with a float ensures that the solution doesn't drop too low and cut off the capillary supply. Roots will eventually grow down into the solution and then you may only need to water once every few weeks but every plant is different.

TRANSFERRING COMPOST-GROWN PLANTS
There is an element of risk when transferring a plant from compost culture – nearly all plants can be grown hydroponically, but success is greater when started from seeds or cuttings. Carefully wash off the soil from established plants without damaging roots. Pour the chosen growing medium around the roots and tap the pot on a table to settle it and support the plant. Initially water from above with half-strength nutrient solution.

GROWING MEDIA
Perlite These tiny bits of expanded rock look like polystyrene. They're cheap, lightweight and reusable as long as you flush them through with a mild bleach solution and then rinse thoroughly. Always water from the top and dampen before use to avoid potentially harmful dust. Good for seeds and cuttings.

Expanded clay lumps (leca pictured) Attractive, lightweight and sterile, these are perfect for indoor plants. Being larger in diameter the capillary action is reduced, so they're not so good for big plants and pots. Water from below if possible.

Rockwool Spun fibres of molten rock made into preformed modules that you soak in water before use. Don't allow them to remain waterlogged and wear gloves as they can irritate the skin.

Greenmix The growing medium of the future; part rockwool, it holds far more moisture around the roots whilst still retaining air. It's more expensive, but well worth it for pricey plants like orchids.

NUTRIENT SOLUTION

This is specially formulated and should be purchased from hydroponic dealers or garden centres. It is normally sold in twin packs that must be made up and applied following the instructions. Ordinary fertilizers for soil culture aren't recommended.

ACTIVE SYSTEMS FOR SERIOUS CROPS
Active systems are scaled-down versions of the ones used by commercial growers. They may seem a bit complicated, but are well worth it if you're serious about growing a decent crop at home (see Buyer's Guide, page 170).

Any plant can be grown hydroponically, but it's a particularly good method for **GROWING INDOOR CROPS**.

FEEDING

WHY FEED?

Plants, like people, need to eat and if you don't feed them they start to look a bit rough and then they get sick. Different plants have different needs, but if you follow these basic rules and check individual plant requirements, you should be alright. If you don't feed, there's no way you can keep plants in good condition.

WHEN TO FEED?

Feed a plant when it's in active growth. For most plants that means between mid spring and mid autumn – when the days are longer and there's more sunshine. Feed much less or not at all in winter.

Potting compost normally contains fertilizers so when you first buy a plant it'll be okay for two or three months and then it'll start getting hungry. That's when you've got to begin feeding, unless it's winter, of course.

Don't feed sick plants, it's a fertilizer, not a medicine and if a plant is under stress already, it won't be able to cope with the additional pressure.

HOW MUCH?

A lot of plants like to be fed once a fortnight, but you won't go far wrong if you feed a plant at half the recommended strength once a week or even every time you water during the growing season. That way you won't forget to do it. In winter, cut it out altogether.

Feeding helps plants to grow vigorously, however, if you don't want your dracaena to outgrow your living room too fast, be a bit tight with the fertilizer.

SIGNS OF UNDERFEEDING

- Growth is slow, the plant barely changes size and pests and diseases take up residence.
- The plant doesn't flower or if it does they're small and pale and you wish it hadn't bothered.
- Stems are weak and lower leaves drop off prematurely.
- Leaves are pale, maybe yellow spotted and generally look sick.

SIGNS OF OVERFEEDING

- Useless, lanky growth particularly in winter.
- Stunted growth in summer.
- A white crust appears on the surface of the compost and the side of terracotta pots.
- Leaves wilt or have crispy brown edges and spotted leaves.

WHAT TO FEED?

Most indoor plant fertilizers are balanced. They include nitrogen for leaves, phosphorus for roots, potassium for flowers and fruit and then there are usually a few trace elements added for all the twiddly bits. Other fertilizers may be top-heavy in one of the main ingredients like tomato fertilizer, which is loaded with potassium but, if in doubt, go for a standard or balanced one.

Liquid feed This is the best and easiest way to give a plant the right amount of fertilizer. Keep it next to your watering can and add a couple of drops to each can of water. Don't pour it onto really dry compost or it can harm the roots by being too concentrated in one area. Water dry compost first. The organic options are seaweed extract, or if you have a wormery in the garden, dilute the liquid that you drain off with ten parts water.

Slow-release feed This comes as special granules which provide a good, steady dose for a whole growing season. Add them to the compost in spring when topdressing or repotting. Bone meal and seaweed meal are organic alternatives. Fish, blood and bone and pelleted chicken poo are also organic, but faster acting.

Tablets and sticks These are glued-together slow-release granules. They do work, but they're a bit gimmicky. The idea that it is a measured dose is a bit daft because they mostly feed the bit of compost that they're stuck into. You can push the tablets down near the roots with the blunt end of a pencil.

Foliar feed This is like a major caffeine injection. It provides instant zap and is perfect if the foliage is looking unhealthy. Mix with water and spray onto the leaves with a hand mister. Good for plants like bromeliads that don't have a lot going on in the root department.

PLANT FOOD The range of fertilizers in garden centres is mind-boggling. To keep things simple, just buy a single bottle of liquid feed.

PROPAGATION

Some people will only ever treat indoor plants as pieces of furniture or part of the decor and will never get very attached to them. But for others it's a different story, and propagating their own indoor plants is likely to be one of their first encounters with gardening proper. In a lot of cases, propagation is a simple and deeply satisfying way to get new plants and, of course, it's virtually free. For others though, propagation is a complete pain in the backside, it takes ages and doesn't really work, so buying a new plant is probably the answer.

WHEN?

The best time of year to do most types of propagation is in spring and early summer. The days are getting longer, there's lots more sunshine and the plants have the whole of the growing season ahead of them in which to make new roots and shoots.

CUTTINGS

This can be the easiest way to get more plants. For some, like tradescantia and ivy, you literally just have to stick a bit in a glass of water on the window-sill and wait for it to root. For others, it's a bit more complicated, but not much.

Fill a pot with seed and cuttings compost (this is important because it must be low in nutrients or else you will get all sorts of problems) and insert the cuttings around the edge. Always use fresh compost because old stuff can contain pests and diseases. To cut down on water loss, poke four sticks into the compost, put a clear polythene bag over the top and fasten it onto the pot with an elastic band. You could use the bottom half of a plastic mineral water bottle instead, but don't cover cacti, succulents or pelargoniums as they don't like the close, humid atmosphere. Put the pot out of the reach of direct sun and remove yellowing leaves. Check them regularly and when new growth appears, water the compost first and pot up the new plants into individual pots, but be really careful not to damage the fragile roots and new shoots.

STEM CUTTINGS

This works for most plants, especially those with soft stems like philodendron. Cut a healthy, sturdy, non-flowering shoot between 8–15cm long (depending on the size of the donor plant). Cut off the leaves on the lower half and trim the stem just below a leaf joint with a razor blade or really sharp knife to avoid crushing the stem. Make a hole in the compost with a dibber or pencil, dip the bottom centimetre in hormone rooting powder, tap off the excess and put the cutting into the hole. Firm it in with your fingertips. Small cuttings like those of *Hoya bella* can be dipped in rooting powder and inserted in cubes of florist's oasis or rockwool and stood on a tray of water but make sure it never runs dry. Once they've rooted, you just pot up the whole thing.

Pelargonium and fuchsia cuttings can be taken in late summer, but woody-stemmed plants like sparmannia should be done in spring. Take a side shoot and tug it downwards to pull it off the main stem with a 'heel' of bark and pot up as above.

LEAF CUTTINGS

Some plants don't have stems at all and the leaves shoot straight out of the crown, level with the compost. These can be propagated from a single leaf or even a piece of leaf and the leaf cuttings will produce lots of tiny new plantlets. When they're big enough to handle, trim off the old leaf and pot up the plants.

Whole leaf With succulents like sedum, crassula and echeveria, take off the leaf and let it dry out a bit for a few days. Cover the compost in sharp sand, push the leaf base into the compost and lean the back of it against the rim of the pot.

Leaf with stalk For leaves that have a stalk, like peperomia and saintpaulia, cut a mature leaf with a razor blade, dip the stalk in hormone rooting powder and insert immediately in the compost.

Parts of leaves Big leaves can be chopped up. Streptocarpus can be cut into 3 or 4 strips, each with a bit of midrib. Place the base of each leaf section into a tray of compost. Sansevieria also can be

LEAF CUTTING (top left) **AIR LAYERING** (top centre) **CANE CUTTING** (top right)
DIVISION (bottom left) **STEM CUTTING** (bottom centre) **OFFSET** (bottom right)

111

PROPAGATION

chopped into 5cm-wide strips, but the new plant will only be variegated if you leave two nibs of the outer yellow part sticking down below (see picture on page 110). As a general rule, variegated plants can't be propagated by leaf cuttings.

CANE CUTTINGS

As they get older, plants that make stiff, erect canes such as yucca, dieffenbachia, dracaena and cordyline lose their lower leaves and look a bit shabby. You've probably seen those ready-to-plant canes or 'Ti plants' in the shops and it's the same idea here. Cut off a section of cane and chop the leafless part into bits about 6–10cm long. Lay them flat, half submerged in the compost and they'll soon sprout. The leafy top section can be used as a stem cutting and the butchered parent plant will soon sprout from just below the wound. You can also put cane cuttings vertically in the compost, but make sure they are the right way up by cutting the bottom at an angle.

OFFSETS

Some parent plants, like bromeliads, cacti and succulents, produce baby plants or offsets at the base. When they're about a quarter the size of the parent plant and beginning to resemble them, trim them off close to the parent stem with a sharp knife and pot up like a cutting. If possible, ensure the offset has some root already.

PLANTLETS

Some plants, like spider plants and saxifrage, produce new plantlets on the end of stems. If they already have short, stubby roots, remove the plantlets and pot up. Otherwise, peg them down into an adjacent fresh pot of compost with a hairpin of stiff wire and separate them once rooted. This works pretty well for trailing plants like ivy, if you peg down the stems.

DIVISION

Clump-forming plants, such as maranta and ophiopogon, can be divided. Take off the pot and carefully tease the clump apart ensuring your new piece of plant has plenty of roots. If there is a main root connecting it to the parent, cut through it with a knife.

AIR LAYERING

This is a good approach when things like rubber plants and cheese plants get leggy or start bashing into the ceiling. About 70–80cm from the tip of the plant, find a bare piece of stem about 10cm below where a leaf joins. Strip a 1cm-wide band of bark off by cutting two shallow rings with a sharp knife. Paint the wound with hormone rooting powder and then get a big handful of really moist sphagnum moss and pack it round the cut. Secure the moss firmly in place with a piece of clear polythene that is then wired onto the stem at the top and bottom. In a couple of months or so you'll see new roots growing in the moss. Cut the stem below the wire, remove the polythene and pot up the new plant. Keep it away from bright sunlight for the first few weeks and be careful not to overwater. The old plant should shoot again, so don't chuck it out.

SEED SOWING

Unlike real gardening, this is definitely not what indoor plants are all about unless you're growing edible stuff. Propagating most indoor plants from seed is difficult and is like watching paint dry except it takes a lot longer. If you must do it follow the instructions on the packet. Different seeds need different techniques, but as a general rule...

Fill trays or pots with seed compost to within 1cm of the rim. Firm it gently with the base of another tray or pot and sprinkle water onto it. Sow seed as directed on the packet and unless very fine, cover with a 1cm layer of sieved compost or vermiculite. Place a sheet of glass on top or seal in a clear polythene bag to make a mini greenhouse. Then put on a window-sill in a centrally heated room at a minimum 20°C. As soon as they sprout, remove the glass or bag and keep out of direct sun. Regularly spray with water and never let them dry out. Turn the pots or trays every couple of days so the seedlings don't bend towards the light. As soon as the seedlings are large enough to handle, hold a leaf and gently tease out the roots with a pencil. Plant them into trays of individual cells or pots and grow on in a bright spot at average room temperature for a few weeks before treating as adults and moving to a more permanent home.

PRUNING (right) actually encourages growth, so don't be afraid to do it, but most indoor plants never need to go under the knife.

PRUNING

Indoor plants don't need a lot of pruning because they just get on and do their thing, but they do sometimes become misshapen. There are two ways to prune: pinching out and cutting back.

PINCHING OUT

This is especially important for fast-growing, soft-stemmed species like tradescantia, coleus, pilea and beloperone to stop them getting lanky. You pinch out or 'stop' a plant by nipping the growing tip between finger and thumb just above a node where leaves join the stem. This tip might only be about 1cm long. Use nails scissors if this is fiddly. Keep pinching throughout the growing period.

CUTTING BACK

If plants are just too big or unbalanced, cut out thick woody stems just above a bud. If a plant like a yucca is already touching the ceiling don't just nip off the top or you'll be pruning it every five minutes. Be brave and chop off 70 or 80cm so it bushes out low down (see Air Layering, page 112). Make sure you cut back at the beginning of the growing season to give the dormant buds time to do their stuff. Use sharp secateurs or scissors so you don't crush the stems and encourage pests and diseases. Some plants, including ficus, bleed sap from cut wounds. You can stem the flow by rubbing bonfire ash, or for that matter cigarette ash, into the cut but wash your hands afterwards because the sap will cause havoc if you get it in your eyes.

DEADHEADING

Flowering goes on for a lot longer if you snip off faded blooms to channel the plant's energy into new buds. Badly timed pruning can stop plants flowering altogether so check in the relevant section before you do it. Remove dead, damaged and yellowing leaves as well, but be careful not to harm the main stem.

WHILE YOU'RE ON HOLIDAY

Most plants won't suffer at all if left for only a week, especially in winter when they aren't growing much anyway. Two weeks is pushing it a bit but three weeks, particularly in summer, is decidedly dodgy. So if you don't get on with the neighbours, you need a plan or your holiday will be like the Grim Reaper.

So after you cancel the milk and check the oven is turned off, give the plants a damn good soaking, move them away from sunny window-sills and group them together in a cool room out of direct sunlight. Keeping them all in the bath is a safe bet, but don't leave them sitting in water as that'll do more harm than good. Instead, stand the plants on pebbles in a water-filled tray. The pebbles raise the plant out of the water which, as it evaporates, raises the humidity around the plant and reduces its thirst. Some plants, like *Ficus benjamina*, hate being moved, so are best left to chance.

Alternatively, you can buy a piece of capillary matting from the garden centre and drape it over your draining board with one end trailing into the water-filled sink. Stand the plants on the matting and the water will be sucked out of the sink and up into the compost. Sadly, this only works for plastic pots because the thicker clay ones don't allow the essential contact between compost and matting. Do a trial run to check your sink is watertight or you could end up with a load of dead plants to welcome you home. You could always rig up the same thing with your toilet cistern because it tops itself up automatically.

You can also buy special wicks, one end of which you drape into a water-filled jar and the other into the compost or drainage hole. Or there are special porous clay bulbs that provide a constant, but limited supply to the compost. Don't fret about watering too much and remember that overwatering is far more likely to harm a plant than letting it go a bit dry for a week or two. In winter, make sure that the plants have got enough warmth while you're away. Don't be miserly and turn off the heating or you'll come back to a lot of very dejected plants.

If you do get back and find your plants have wilted, follow the advice in Bringing them back from the dead, page 117.

GIVE THE PLANTS A BREAK

Most indoor plants could do with a holiday too. Usually in winter they have a dormant period of R and R when they take some time out from all that growing. Some plants will let you know when they're ready by shedding their leaves or even dying down, but a lot of foliage plants aren't quite so communicative. You have to take your cue from the lower light levels and the shorter days of winter. The plant will stop growing and it's really important that you cut right down on feeding and watering and, if possible, lower the temperature by moving to a cooler room. Winter-blooming plants are the exception to this because they mostly need watering and feeding before and during flowering.

In summer, take your plants outside. The rain will wash layers of dust off the leaves, making the whole plant look happier and letting more light through to the leaf surface. Make sure they are in shade though, perhaps under a tree, or the massive increase in sunshine will scorch and bleach the leaves. Yuccas are a prime example, the leaves go a whitish brown in the sun.

GERBERAS are amongst the best air purifiers. They need watering plentifully during the growing season and shouldn't be allowed to dry out while you're on holiday.

BRINGING THEM BACK
FROM THE DEAD

Technically this plant has reached the Permanent Wilting Point and must suffer **THE ULTIMATE SOLUTION**.

DRIED-OUT PLANTS

If you've forgotten to water a plant it will usually wilt with the leaves drooping dejectedly. On top of that, the compost shrinks so when you add water it refuses to rehydrate and the water just pours down the sides without soaking in. Plunge the whole pot into a bucket of water and hold it under until all the air bubbles have escaped. Scrape out the top layer of compost and replace it with fresh, poking it loosely down the sides with your fingertips. The next few times you water it, add a couple of drops of washing-up liquid to act as a wetting agent and the old compost will eventually rehydrate. Then you can carry on watering as normal. If a wilted plant hasn't picked up noticeably in a couple of hours, you're probably looking at the ultimate solution.

Sometimes soil-based compost won't absorb water even though it hasn't dried out. Break up the hard surface with a screwdriver, being careful not to damage the roots, and immerse in water as above.

DUSTING AND SHINING

Dusty leaves look horrid, sunlight can't be absorbed for photosynthesis and their pores get clogged up so that the plants can't breathe properly. Support a leaf with your hand and wipe it with a wet sponge. Better still, put them in the shower and rinse it all off.

There is something of an obsession with leaf shine, which actually tends to make plants look plasticky and artificial. If you must do this, make sure you hold the nozzle of the aerosol at least 30cm from the leaf or the freezing propellant will damage the leaves. Leaf shine wipes are good because they clean the leaf at the same time. Some people use beer, milk and olive oil, but they should be stopped as these are all potentially harmful. Never shine ferns, palms, cacti, succulents and things with hairy leaves because it can kill them. You can remove dust from cacti and hairy leaves with a soft paintbrush.

DISPOSABLE PLANTS

Some plants must be treated as temporary. Like a bunch of flowers, they should just be chucked straight onto the compost heap once they're past their best. Certain flowering plants are prime candidates, as soon as they've bloomed – out they go. Otherwise you have to nurse them back into flower over the next 10 months during which time they'll just sit there looking back at you, begging to be put out of their misery and making your room look untidy (see the relevant plant section).

SOME PLANTS ARE FOR CHRISTMAS, NOT FOR LIFE

Some winter-flowering plants are traditionally sold at Christmas and Easter. They look good for a month or two and then you have to decide whether to keep them or not.

Poinsettia These are vile plants with large red modified leaves or bracts (the actual flowers are small, yellow things) that now come in white and a revolting pink. Well-heated rooms and draughts will make them wilt, so place them on a pebble tray to keep the humidity high and let them dry out a bit between waterings. Put them in a bright spot, give a weak feed occasionally and they'll last for three months.

To get them to produce their coloured bracts next year you'll need to give them about 14 hours of total darkness followed by 10 hours of daylight every day from early autumn for eight weeks. How very annoying. It's much easier to chuck it away and get another one next year.

Cyclamen Like African violets, these are old people's plants that remind you of granny. High temperatures and lack of water will make them wilt so ideally keep them in a cool room or on a cool window-sill at between 5–16°C. Lots of light and a weekly feed should keep them flowering for months. When they've finished, let the corm (the bulb thing) dry out completely until late summer, repot and start to water again. Watch out for vine weevils.

Azalea Draughts, erratic watering and droughts make the leaves fall off. Hot, dry rooms and radiators can also kill so 10–15°C is best. Water regularly by plunging the pot in a bucket until air bubbles stop escaping from the compost. You'll probably need to water three times a week, but avoid hard water (see Water, page 96). Remove flowers as they fade and they'll go on for a month or so.

Start to feed weekly after flowering and put outside in a bit of shade after the last frosts of spring. Sink the pot into the ground to stop it from drying out and bring back in before the first frosts of winter. It should flower again the following spring.

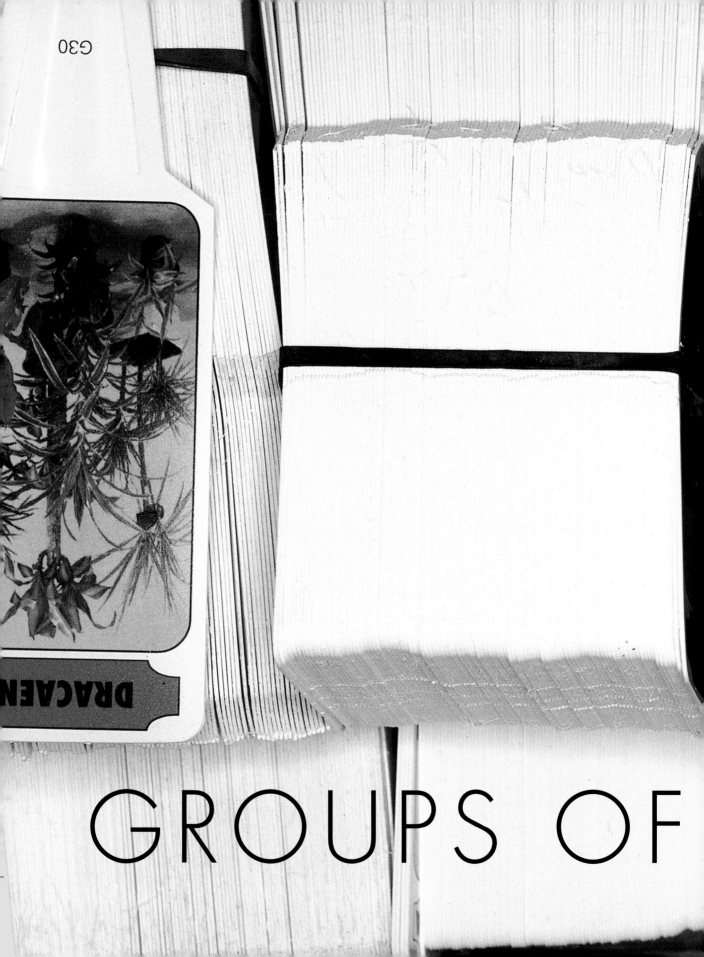

G30

DRACAEN

GROUPS OF

G90

1353

PLANTS

HERBS + EDIBLES

If you fancy yourself as a bit of whiz in the kitchen, there is nothing better than growing your own ingredients and being able to pick fresh herbs and vegetables straight from the window-sill. Most edibles are better off outside or in a greenhouse but if you don't have that choice these ones are worth a try indoors.

HERBS

Herbs should be treated as short-lived plants indoors. Some are annuals anyway and even the shrubby ones gradually peter out and the fact that you're obviously going to pull leaves off them doesn't help. But being easy to replace and grow, this isn't a problem. Some can be grown from seed (see Propagation, page 111) but all can be bought as plants from the garden centre to save time and fuss. Those pots of ready-growing herb seedlings from the supermarket are packed in so tightly and pumped so full of fertilizer that they have a very short life span so don't be disappointed when they meet their maker.

Grow on an east- or west-facing window-sill that gets lots of light. Full midday sun will be a bit hot and they'll suffer. Feed fortnightly in summer and always keep the soil moist, but do not overwater. Winter is a not a happy time for herbs because of the shorter days and lower light levels and you may be better off starting again in spring.

Basil is a must for Italian food lovers. You tend to get through quite a lot so you might need a few plants. If you grow it from seed, keep sowing every few weeks between spring and summer because plants don't last very long. Remove any flowers or the plants give up. Keep moist.

Coriander is for fish and curryholics and, like basil, you can make several sowings. Keep cutting and don't let it flower.

Parsley can also be grown from seed but unfortunately it's never wonderfully happy indoors.

Mint should be bought as a growing plant or a little clump can be lifted from the garden. Stand the pot in a saucer of water during summer but keep it drier in winter.

Chives, like mint, can be divided from a clump in the garden. Snip the leaves right down to the base when using it. Even the flowers can be eaten in salads.

HERBS (above) need a window-sill with lots of light but don't let them get frazzled by too much midday sun.
MINT TEA (right). Mint is really easy to grow if you stand it in a saucer of water.

Thyme likes a bit of grit or sand mixed into the compost and can stomach more sunshine and drought than most. It should never be stood in water and likes a scattering of garden lime added to the compost as a one-off fertilizer. Trim over with shears in spring.

Oregano, and **marjoram** which is a close relative, **tarragon** and **sage** can all be grown on a cool bright window-sill. The compost should be kept slightly moist and you can feed every fortnight with half-strength liquid feed. If you overfeed, the new growth is very leggy and weedy unless the light levels are very good.

Lemon grass is really easy to grow but you need to buy the stems as fresh and intact as possible. Unfortunately the base is always trimmed off the ones in the shops and if too much has been removed they won't root. Stand the thick end in a glass of water on a sunny window-sill. After a week or so, stubby roots should appear, so pot it up into compost. Keep moist and feed every other week once it's started sprouting leaves. A spring-grown stem should make a nice grassy clump by autumn and the following spring you can start harvesting stems for your Thai cooking.

SALAD AND VEG

Sow on a window-sill from early to mid spring or buy young plants. Give them lots of light, water and a fortnightly dose of tomato-like fertilizer once they're about a month old. Watch out for whitefly.

Tomatoes need to be kept moist and fed weekly with a tomato fertilizer. There are a few small varieties that do ok indoors such as Tumbler, Minibel, Santa Fi and Brasero.

Aubergines are quite small plants about 40cm tall. They may need staking and the leaves should be misted regularly.

Cucumbers aren't often grown indoors but the variety Fembaby is a small 90cm plant that can be grown up a cane and will produce several fruit. Stand in a saucer of water and mist daily.

Sweet peppers and **chilli peppers** are worth growing and, although they don't excel, you can still get a useful crop. Green peppers are just unripe red ones. Choose a small variety.

Okra, or lady's fingers, are used in Indian food and is surprisingly easy to grow. It reaches about 80cm and has pretty hollyhock-like flowers and interesting fruit.

SEEDS AND BEANS

Mustard and cress, like many sprouted seeds, are not only tasty but very nutritious. Sow cress evenly on soggy kitchen paper or loo roll in a shallow tray and place in a dimly lit spot. Three days later sow the quicker-growing mustard alongside. When they start to sprout, move to a window-sill and harvest a week later.

Bean sprouts, usually mung beans, are dead easy. Soak overnight in water and place in a single layer in a shallow tray and put somewhere warm and dark like the airing cupboard. Sprinkle with water every day and harvest in about a week when they're about 5cm long. If you leave them too long they lose their taste.

Wheat grass looks fantastic growing on the window-sill and its juice is a great natural medicine, which can be used for detoxing and for hangovers. It is also being researched as a possible complementary treatment for cancer. Buy seed from health food shops, or you can buy a wheat grass kit. Rinse and soak the seed in cold water for 12 hours. Sprinkle seeds on a 5cm layer of organic compost in a seed tray and pat down. Cover with a bin liner put in a warm cupboard and water sparingly. Once they sprout, bring them into the light and watch the grass shoot up. You will need a special juicer to extract the juice. (See Suppliers, page 173 for details).

FRUITS AND THINGS

These are familiar items worth diverting from your shopping trolley to a pot of compost on the window-sill. Most won't actually fruit unless you've got a warm conservatory but they do make excellent and unusual indoor plants, and it's nice to see where some of these things come from.

Avocado stones must be soaked for 48 hours in tepid water in a container on a radiator. Suspend the stone, pointy end up, over a jam jar of water by shoving four toothpicks or cocktail sticks into the sides. The base of the stone should just be submerged. Put in a warm dark cupboard. When a shoot appears, between 10 days and five weeks later, move the jar onto a window-sill and once the root almost fills it, transfer to a pot of compost. The pointy bit should just be visible. Once the main shoot reaches 15cm snip a third off. Repot after about two months, water regularly and feed every two weeks in summer. Keep pinching out the tips or it will get tall and leggy. A cane might be needed for support.

Papaya or paw paw turn into good-looking upright plants. Scoop out the black seeds, wash and dry them and plant a few in a pot. Once they've sprouted, thin them to one per pot and give average

COURGETTE FLOWERS (far left). Small varieties of squashes and cucumbers will live happily on a sunny window-sill.
SOME HERBS (left) like coriander and basil don't live for long, so keep growing new plants from seed.
MUSTARD AND CRESS (below) is a rite of passage for most gardeners.

warmth and lots of light. In a warm greenhouse they may fruit. Male and female on separate plants need to be cross-pollinated.

Dates grow on massive palm trees so you're clearly not going to get an adult plant with a crop but what the hell. Eat a date and spit out the stone, wash off any unpleasantness and rub the whole surface with sandpaper so that moisture can get in. Seal it in a bag of damp compost and put it in a warm dark place like an airing cupboard. It might take weeks but once a root appears at the end, plant 2cm deep in a pot of compost and put on a warm, light window-sill. As they grow repot into bigger pots of soil-based compost. Water regularly.

Coffee bushes are often grown as indoor plants in America. They have lovely shiny green leaves and in the third year beautiful fragrant white flowers followed by green berries that ripen to red and contain two seed beans. Eventually you should be able to get enough for at least one cup of coffee. You need to scrounge some unroasted beans from a grocer who roasts and grinds his own coffee. Sow 1cm deep in compost in July on a warm window-sill and cover with paper. Keep at about 16°C in winter and average room temperature in summer.

Sweet potatoes or yams are actually lovely climbing plants related to morning glory. Bury a couple of tubers on their sides in a pot of compost about 3cm below the surface. Put them somewhere as close to 18°C as you can. When the shoots appear, reduce them to two or three and chuck a few more centimetres of compost on top for good measure. They will grow quite quickly. Keep compost moist. They might flower but you're unlikely to get an edible crop of tubers.

Pineapple Buy a fresh pineapple with a really healthy looking crown of leaves on top. Slice off the crown with 1cm of flesh attached and leave it on its side to dry for a few days. Bury the fleshy bit into compost mixed with 25 per cent sharp sand, seal the whole lot in a clear polythene bag and place on a window-sill away from direct sun. When you see new growth sprouting from the centre of the rosette of leaves move to a really sunny spot. Pineapples will only fruit after two or three years in a warm conservatory. Water and feed regularly.

Mangos are huge tropical trees. Wash the seed of a very ripe fruit. Rub it all over with sandpaper and soak the stone in water for two

MOST HERBS AND EDIBLES (above right) can be grown from seed.
CUCUMBERS (left) and squashes prefer a greenhouse, but small varieties will grow on your window-sill.

weeks. Put the bowl in a warm place and change the water every day or it will go smelly. Plant about 3cm deep in a pot of compost, water really well, seal in a polythene bag and put it somewhere warm like the airing cupboard. As soon as it sprouts, take off the bag and put on a warm, sunny window-sill. Regularly repot and pinch out the tips to keep it bushy. Feed every two weeks.

Monkey nuts or peanuts. You need fresh ones still in their shells for this. Crack them slightly and plant three or four close together about 1cm deep in a pot. Seal in a polythene bag and put in the airing cupboard or a heated propagator. After about two weeks when they've sprouted, take the bag off and place on a sunny window-sill. Pot on as a clump into a 30cm-wide pot. Yellow flowers appear in summer followed by downward-facing pods which plunge themselves into the ground and turn into the familiar monkey nuts in autumn. They must never be fed.

Root ginger Buy a really fresh piece of root from a greengrocer. You don't need much – about 5cm. Treat it like a monkey nut but give it loads of water and feed fortnightly with a tomato fertilizer. It will grow about 1.5m and have a beautiful pink flower in summer. They prefer a warm conservatory and don't like direct sunlight.

You can also try growing **lychees**, **olives** and anything else you that takes your fancy.

A CARPET OF WHEAT GRASS (right) looks amazing and it'll cure your hangover. Allegedly.
OLIVE TREES (below) can be brought indoors for a few weeks but are more at home in the garden or conservatory.

CITRUS

You can easily grow your own lemon for a vodka and tonic as long as you have the right conditions in your home and follow some basic guidelines. Somehow, they'll never be quite as good as the imported fruit in the shops but if you grow your own tangerine you'll be so smug it won't matter.

The sweet-scented, usually white, star-shaped flowers are a couple of centimetres wide. They normally bloom in late spring and summer but occasional flowers appear at any time. In the right conditions, lemons and limes can flower almost continuously which makes them the best types to grow and you often get flowers and fruit on the bush at the same time. The fruits are green at first before spending as much as three months ripening to yellow, orange and, er, green. They can then last several months.

SHORTCUTS TO SUCCESS
- Water carefully, overdoing it is the biggest problem.
- Draught-free conditions in winter.
- Ventilate well or put outside in summer.
- Plenty of feeding.
- Cool but not cold in winter.

THE BASICS
Watering Get this wrong and you're stuffed, get it right and you're virtually home and dry. Use tap water, not softened water. Completely soak the thing so water pours out the bottom of the pot into the saucer and let the top 5cm of compost dry out between waterings until the leaves look slightly stressed. If in doubt leave it because overwatering is a killer. Never let it stand in water. In winter, when the plant is resting, water very, very occasionally to stop the compost from drying out totally.

Temperature In summer normal room temperature will do but they're much better off outside or by a permanently open window. In winter, they like to be cool but not cold. This means between 4–10°C, so if you've got an unheated room with a south-facing window you're in luck, otherwise a porch or a heated greenhouse or conservatory will do. Avoid draughts.

Humidity If too low, especially in warmer temperatures, red spider mite can be a problem. Stand in a water-filled tray and raise it up on a 5–8cm layer of gravel so the roots aren't in the water.

SOMEHOW THE FRUIT (above) is never quite as pristine as it is in the shops, but who cares.
CITRUS FRUIT (left) need regular feeding and a cool winter rest.

129

CITRUS

Feeding Citrus are greedy plants. Between spring and autumn, give a high-potash, tomato-type fertilizer every two weeks or when you water. In winter, a fortnightly foliar feed increases fruit set. Mottled yellow leaves is usually a magnesium deficiency cured by watering on sequestered iron, a readily available plant food.

Light In summer citrus yearn to be outdoors in bright light. After the late frosts, start in shade and creep into sunshine over a week. Bring them inside in autumn before the frosts start. They need at least four hours of direct sunlight each day and indoors the sunniest place is probably best for them especially in winter.

Repotting A soil- or loam-based compost is best. Each spring move up one size until you get to a convenient size for your space. *Citrus mitis* will flower and fruit in a little 13 or 15cm pot but most won't do the business until they've grown into a pot at least 25cm wide.

Pruning Very little is needed but branches can get a bit spindly. Shorten long branches by at least half in early spring. Nip out growing tips at any time during spring and summer to make the plant more bushy.

Propagation Cuttings can be taken in late spring and should root after 6 or 8 weeks. Start feeding when new shoots appear and move to brighter light.

VARIETIES

CITRUS MITIS (X *Citrofortunella microcarpa*) the Calomondin orange, makes a virtually spineless 1.2m bush and is one of the easiest citrus to get hold of and grow. It's popular because it flowers

NING
MPER WITH COIN BOXES
S AS THEY ARE WIRED
IC ALARM SYSTEM

sporadically and bears loads of small bright orange fruit throughout the year even when the plant is still tiny. The bitter fruit can be used for marmalade.

MEYER'S LEMON *C. x meyeri* 'Meyer' has thin-skinned pale yellow fruit 7.5cm in diameter but can be tricky. The 'QUATRE SAISONS' lemon variety, now known as 'GAREY'S EUREKA' is much easier.

'WEST INDIAN' is a spicy lime suitable for a rum punch and 'KAFFIR' leaves are essential in Thai cooking. 'TAHITI' is a good lime for beginners.

The OTAHEITE ORANGE, *C. limonia*, is a cross between a lemon and a mandarin and has purple-tinged flowers and yellow or orange fruit.

The SWEET or NAVEL ORANGE *C.sinensis* 'Washington' growing to about 1.2m is just about the only one you can have indoors which is actually sweet tasting. It flowers in spring and fruits in winter.

CLEMENTINES, MANDARIN, TANGERINE and SATSUMA are too big for a house and need a conservatory.

KUMQUAT is not really a citrus but it can be grown in the same way.

TROUBLESHOOTING

- No flowers and therefore no fruit is usually due to poor cultural conditions – lack of light and fertilizer and incorrect watering.
- Discoloration of leaves can be caused by either overwatering or underfeeding.
- Leaf drop is caused by warmth and too moist soil in winter.
- Red spider mite and scale insects are the biggest problems. Wash leaves with a mild solution of washing-up liquid and water to keep them at bay. Mealy bugs, aphids, whitefly can be kept in check the same way. Wipe off honeydew and sooty mould.

LEMONS AND LIMES (left and above) are the best because they can flower and fruit almost continuously.
Apart from being pretty handy for your gin and tonic, they are actually good-looking plants.

BROMELIADS

Bromeliads are smart plants because they've figured out how to absorb food and moisture through their leaves as well as their roots. They mostly come from the jungles of North, Central and South America. Many are epiphytic and live up in the trees, taking nourishment from the atmosphere – hence 'air plants'. Most of the ones grown as indoor plants are stemless with strap-shaped, leathery arching leaves arranged in a rosette and often have a watertight vase at the centre which collects rainwater and dew. Some have both. Many varieties can flower at any time after two or three years when the plant is mature and then the parent produces offsets and slowly dies.

SHORTCUTS TO SUCCESS

- Average room temperature is perfect but over 23°C is more likely to induce flowering.
- Bright light but out of strong direct sunlight. (Ananas and cryptanthus like full sun).
- Keep the central vase topped up with water if there is one and keep compost on the dry side.

THE BASICS

Watering Keep the central vase filled if there is one. Use rainwater in hard-water areas. Empty and refill every two months so it doesn't get stale. Let the compost dry out between waterings but with non-vase types keep compost moist but never soggy.

Light A brightly lit spot is essential but generally those with thicker leathery leaves need more light (including a few hours of direct sun) than those with softer leaves. Give them an occasional shower with rainwater to wash dust off the leaves.

Temperature Normal warm room temperatures will do for most bromeliads and it shouldn't drop below 13°C. To get them to flower though, you may have to crank the heating up to about 23 or 24°C. Raise humidity, especially in centrally heated rooms, by placing on a pebble tray. Air plants need almost daily misting with water.

Feeding Every three or four weeks, spray a dilute liquid feed at half recommended strength, onto the leaves, compost and central vase.

Keep the central rosette of **GUZMANIA CONIFERA** (above) topped up with water, except when in flower.
VRIESIAS have flattened flower spikes and many **GUZMANIAS** have elongated rosettes (right).

Repotting Most don't need repotting due to their puny root systems. Largest pot size needed is often about 13cm.

Propagation Offsets appear at the base after the main plant has flowered which then starts to die off. When the offsets have stopped being elongated and start to resemble the parent, cut them off with a knife. They should have some roots attached so check before you do it. Plant shallowly in cuttings compost, enclose in a polythene bag and keep warm until established.

VARIETIES

AECHMEA The most common one, *A.fasciata*, with its alien pink flower-head and wide grey leaves has been consigned to the Kitsch section (pages 34–39).

AIR PLANTS – TILLANDSIA These mostly have grey-green furry scales that absorb water from humid air and nutrients from airborne dust. *Tillandsia usneoides* is the Spanish moss that hangs in great curtains from trees in the Florida everglades and would make a fantastic organic shower curtain. *T. ionantha* is only about 8cm tall and, like many of the other species, has a pretty flower spike. *T. cyanea*, with its big pink flowerhead, needs compost and a pot. Mist air plants almost daily with water or they won't survive, especially in heated rooms. Brightly lit bathrooms are the best environment.

NEOREGELIA The dramatic blushing bromeliad, *Neoregelia carolinae* 'Marechalii' stands nearly 20cm tall. It has glossy leaves about 20–25cm long and, just before the small lavender-coloured flowers appear in the central watertight vase, all the inner leaves turn a brilliant red colour for several months. The curiously popular cream and green striped *N. carolinae f. tricolor* is a real eighties' plant and looks like it's made of plastic. Neoregelias like brighter sun than many bromeliads and a liquid and foliar feed every two or three weeks.

NIDULARIUM These are really similar to neoregelia but often have small spines on the edges of the leaves. High humidity is needed.

GUZMANIA The scarlet star is probably vying for the title of world's most popular bromeliad. There are lots of species available including *G. lingulata minor* which has red and orange bracts which shoot up from the centre and produces small yellow flowers. Keep the compost moist and temperatures ideally above 18°C.

VRIESEA The flaming sword, *Vriesea splendens*, is something of a double whammy with exotic purple banded leaves and a sumptuous red flower spike up to 60cm tall. A little direct sunlight is needed to induce them to flower but avoid strong midday summer sun.

BILLBERGIA Definitely the easiest bromeliad to grow indoors, some of these will survive temperatures down to just above freezing and flower while still very young. *B. nutans* is the one you come across most. The 30cm-long green leaves are a bit wild and sometimes turn red in full sunlight and the yellowy green flowers are backed by 8cm-long pink bracts. They flower at any time of year and grow continuously if warm enough.

CRYPTANTHUS The earth stars are ground-hugging plants, often as little as 10cm across, and grown for their stripy or banded leaves rather than flowers. *C. bromelioides tricolor* is beautiful with cream and green striped leaves with a pink edge. Annoyingly, it is the hardest to grow because it can wither and die just for the hell of it.

They often have only five or six leaves and no central vase. They need loads of light but very little watering or feeding.

ANANAS You can only grow edible pineapples indoors if you've got a heated greenhouse. But there are a couple of varieties with green, cream or white striped leaves and inedible pink fruits on long flower spikes. *A. bracteatus striatus*, the red pineapple, is a compact 50cm in diameter. Sun improves leaf colour but it's hard to get them to flower and fruit indoors so buy them when they are.

TROUBLESHOOTING

- Pale brown patches can be caused by scorch from the sun.
- Brown leaf tips caused by lack of humidity in dry rooms or underwatering of central vase.
- Watch out for scale and mealy bug.
- Plants dry out and shrivel if underwatered or in poor light and cold rooms.

GUZMANIA (left) with its tall spike of coloured bracts must be the world's most popular bromeliad.
At flowering time, the central leaves of **NEOREGELIA** and **NIDULARIUM** (below left) turn deep pink or red.
TILLANDSIA CYANEA (below right) unlike most of the 'air plant' species needs to be grown in a pot.

ORCHIDS

Orchids have an erotic, exotic fascination. Collectors will pay fortunes for rare specimens and people have killed for them. Most of the 1,000s of different species and hybrids grow from egg-shaped pseudobulbs which give rise to the name orchid from the Greek meaning testicle. Each swollen water-storing stem that emerges from the pseudobulb flowers once, withers and dies. Most need the controlled environment of a greenhouse or conservatory to survive but there are at least five groups or genera that will be happy in your living room and some will even thrive.

SHORTCUTS TO SUCCESS

- Avoid overwatering, only water moderately.
- Humidity must be high.
- Bright filtered light is needed for most species.
- Keep a close eye on the temperature.

THE BASICS

Light Orchids need bright filtered light so grow near a window, but avoid direct summer sun. In winter move orchids to a really bright window and if possible give supplementary artificial lighting to stretch day length to 10 hours and improve flowering.

Temperature A steady temperature is needed to ensure flowering. As a general rule stick to 20°C in summer and 15°C in winter. At night they must have a slightly cooler temperature about 5°C less. Check with a thermometer. High humidity is essential, stand plants in pebble trays and hose down the floor of conservatories and green houses daily.

Water Overwatering is the most common problem. Moderate watering once a week is usually plenty, letting at least the top half of potting mixture dry out in between. In their brief winter rest period let them dry out almost totally. Use soft, tepid water; rainwater is good. Cold water can shock them.

Feed Give a weak foliar feed about once a month or every third or fourth watering but not during rest periods. Overfed plants produce lots of leaves but no flowers.

Potting Excellent drainage is essential. Grow in two parts rockwool or shredded bark to one part sphagnum moss and one of lime-free sand or

The **SLIPPER ORCHID** flower (above), *Paphiopedilum callosum*, lasts two or three months between autumn and spring.
ORCHID flowers (left) follow the same pattern with the same number of petals, but there are thousands of variations.

ORCHIDS

perlite with a little added charcoal to absorb toxins. Premixed bags are readily available. Put 5cm of broken terracotta pots in the bottom of a plastic pot for drainage. Repot every other year in spring, carefully removing any old potting mixture. Shake new potting mixture around the roots and poke it down carefully with a pencil. Newly potted plants should only be sprayed and not watered for the first month.

Propagation Divide into clumps of two or three pseudobulbs and repot as above. The stem types can be propagated from stem tip cuttings or side shoots taken with at least two aerial roots.

Resting period Most orchids need a rest period in order to flower well. This may only last for a few weeks and is indicated in some species by leaves dying back. The temperature should be lowered by about 5°C and watering decreased until the potting mixture dries out.

EASY VARIETIES

CYMBIDIUM are the easiest and best for virgin growers but they get more hungry and thirsty than most. Easily recognized by a clump of tall leaves about 40cm high, the plants need a short rest in autumn.

PHALAENOPSIS, the moth orchid, is also very easy to grow. A steady minimum temperature of 20°C is important. Shorten stems of dead flowers to just below the lowest bloom and new ones will grow on side shoots. They'll flower almost all year.

ODONTOGLOSSUM GRANDE, the tiger orchid, has bright yellow and rusty brown flowers about 17 or 18cm across from late summer to late autumn. They need a constant temperature of 15°C and a high humidity. Repot annually and divide large clumps.

COELOGYNE Mature plants produce lots of fragrant flowers in winter and early spring and the easiest is *C. cristata*. Water plentifully keeping potting mixture thoroughly moist and give a winter rest period. Rarely needs repotting.

PAPHIOPEDILUM The lone flowers of the slipper orchid, called so because the pouch-shaped lip looks like a moccasin, last between eight and twelve weeks and appear between autumn and spring. Give medium light, never direct sun and supplementary light in winter to promote flowering. They don't have a proper rest period but cut watering right down for six weeks after flowering.

Some **ODONTOGLOSSUM** (above) can flower almost continuously under the right conditions as long as the humidity is kept up.
PHALAENOPSIS (right), the flat-faced moth orchid – one of the easiest to grow in your living room and can flower nearly all year.

CACTI

Cacti are by far the easiest plants to grow indoors. They are tough, virtually indestructible, Schwarzeneggers of the plant world. They're specially adapted to cope with neglect and it is possible to keep certain cacti alive for over a year without even watering. Sure they won't grow at all, in fact they'll be hang gliding over the abyss of death but add water and they'll soak it up like a sponge and burst into life. This is good news for us as keepers of plants because they're guilt free. But in order to thrive, they must be watered and fed regularly during summer and this is where most people go wrong.

Plants usually lose water through their leaves so the cactus has cleverly got rid of them and the job of photosynthesis is done by the swollen stem. All cacti are succulents but not all succulents are cacti. Cacti have areoles from which sprout tufts of spines, bristles or hairs but if a succulent has spines they grow straight from the stem like the thorns on a rose. Most cacti come from the Americas and there are two kinds: those from the desert and those from the tropical jungle.

Coloured stems are sometimes grafted onto other cacti and **FAKE PAPER FLOWERS** are stuck in the top (above). Don't be fooled.
MAMMILLARIA MICROHELIA (left) Lots of sun, some food and water and you can't go wrong with cacti.

141

SHORTCUTS TO SUCCESS

- Full sunshine is essential all year.
- Feed and water regularly in summer and neglect them a bit in winter.
- Keep the plant slightly pot-bound.
- Give a slightly cooler temperature in winter.

DESERT CACTI

The flowering period may be over months, but individual flowers only last for a day. They may be red to pink, white, yellow or orange and trumpet or bell-shaped with petals. Some, including echinopsis and cereus, bloom at night and are scented but most cacti flowers don't smell. Most should start flowering after three or four years.

Light Give them the sunniest place in the house. In summer you can stick them on your balcony or patio, but remember the more sun they get, the more water they'll need. Rotate plants occasionally.

Temperature Normal room temperature is fine but in winter, most, apart from the hairy types, like to rest at 5°C, preferably in an unheated room, glazed porch or on a cool window-sill away from radiators. The hairy cacti *Cephalocereus senilis* and *Espostoa lanata* need a minimum winter temp of 15°C.

Watering In spring and summer soak the compost thoroughly every week or two letting the top bit dry out between waterings. Avoid splashing the stems. In winter, while they're resting, the compost should be dry or the roots will rot. But in heated rooms, water a little bit once a month to stop them from shrivelling.

Feeding Feed once a fortnight with a high-potassium, tomato-type fertilizer to encourage flowers. High-nitrogen fertilizers can make plants leggy and flabby and should be avoided. Never feed in winter.

Potting and repotting Cacti must have compost that doesn't hold too much water. Mix two parts loam, peat-based or peat-free compost mixed with one part perlite, sharp sand or fine grit for drainage. Most cacti don't mind being a little pot-bound. Repot every other year at any time except winter. Wrap a piece of folded newspaper around the plant to hold it or fashion a pair of tongs from a really stiff cardboard box. Remove the pot and shake as much compost off the roots as possible without causing damage and either replace in the same pot or move up one size.

Propagation Take cuttings in spring or summer. Some cacti produce offsets at the base and others, like opuntia, are segmented or branched. Dry the cutting for a couple of days so the cut surface doesn't rot, and stick it into some compost.

CACTI

For non-branching columnar types, like cereus, cut at least 5cm off the tip of the stem and root as above. Shoots will appear around the cut of the parent plant and these can be removed and potted up once they've reached 5cm.

Pests, diseases and problems Watch out for mealy bug, scale and red spider mite and if you put them outside in summer, smear the side of the pot with grease to ward off slugs. Dust can be cleaned off with a paintbrush. Weedy, lanky stems are caused by too much heat in winter or too little light in summer. Localized corky patches are caused by physical damage, insects and sudden cold. Soft, brown patches are caused by stem rot disease. Cut out infected tissue and drench compost with a fungicide such as carbendazim. Lack of growth is usually due to underwatering and underfeeding in summer.

JUNGLE CACTI

These are a number of different species, including the ones you get at Christmas and Easter, with flattened trailing stems and showy pink or red flowers. Avoid strong sunlight at all times of year. Keep the humidity up and feed with high-potassium, tomato-like fertilizer from the moment the flower buds form until the last bloom fades. After flowering let them rest for a couple of months at a cooler temperature of 13–15°C, cut down watering and stop feeding. In the summer, put them outside in the shade.

ECHINOCACTUS GRUSONII (left) The bigger the better as far as the golden barrel cactus is concerned.
CEREUS JAMACARU (below) is a proper desert cactus that would make Sergio Leone proud.

SUCCULENTS

Succulents, as luck would have it, are specially adapted to cope with neglect. They've developed cunning ways to combat drought by storing water in plump fleshy leaves and thick juicy stems. But just because they take a long time to die of thirst doesn't mean they don't need water and food. Like cacti, which are a distinct group of succulents, they need regular watering right through the growing season and then to be kept drier and cooler in winter. They come in all sorts of shapes with attractive stems and leaves but they can also be coaxed into flowering if you treat them right.

SHORTCUTS TO SUCCESS
- Average room temperature from spring to autumn. Cooler in winter. • Full sunshine for most varieties.
- Feed during active growth. • Avoid very cold water or dramatic chills.

EUPHORBIA TRICHOMANIA 'RED' (above left). The leaflets fall off with age and this thorny plant becomes a impostor.
The ZEBRA HAWORTHIA (above right) is incredibly tough and never needs feeding.
ALOE VERA (right) grows well on a window-sill. Break off a leaf and squeeze the soothing gel onto scalds and burns.

Many **ECHEVERIAS**, like *E.* 'Perle von Nürnberg' (above) have a pale white bloom on the leaves that is damaged by touch.
The **GHOST PALM** (right), *Pachypodium lameri*, can easily grow to 2m tall.
ALOES (far right) will grow in cool or warm rooms and only need feeding a couple of times a year.

THE BASICS

Light Succulents need as much as possible so basically a really sunny window-sill. Give them a regular quarter turn so they don't develop a Pisa-like lean towards the light. In summer put them outside. Aloes, gasterias and haworthias don't like direct sunshine.

Temperature The warmth and low humidity of a living room is perfect for most succulents but a slightly cooler temperature in winter helps them to flower well.

Watering While they're growing between spring and autumn they actually need watering quite a lot. But the fleshy leaves are easily damaged by splashes so water from the bottom. Stand the pot in a tray of water about 5cm deep and let it suck it up by capillary action until the top of the compost is moist. Never let succulents remain standing in water. Allow the top 2cm of compost to dry out before you water again.

Feeding Give an ordinary liquid feed at slightly less than full strength once every two weeks. Don't overdo it or you'll get soft, weak growth and they won't flower.

Potting and repotting Drainage is paramount. Use any container as long as it has lots of holes in the bottom. Clay pots need a few crocks of broken terracotta at the base. Repot annually or every other year depending on how fast it grows. Use a potting mixture made up of at least one part sharp sand to two parts loam or peat-free compost.

Propagation Many produce offsets at the base that can be carefully pulled away and simply planted up. They'll soon develop roots. Branching types can be treated in the same way; cut off a small branch and, if necessary, support it with a small stick. Others are propagated easily by leaf cuttings. Dry cuttings for a couple of days and then lay them on the surface of the moist compost or bury the cut ends (see Propagation, page 110).

Pests and diseases Watch out for mealy bugs between leaves. They also live on the roots so keep an eye out when repotting. Plants put outside for the summer can be devastated by slugs and snails. Smear the edge of the pot with grease to stop them.

VARIETIES

AEONIUM ARBOREUM ATROPURPUREUM has rosettes of deep purple leaves and turns into a miniature tree. They need lots of light all year. Smaller varieties of **AGAVE** like the *A. Victoriae-reginae* and *A. filifera* are best indoors (see Outside In, p166–169). **ALOE VARIEGATA**, the partridge-breasted aloe has rosettes of thick dark green leaves with white bands. Spikes of tubular flowers appear in late winter. **ALOE VERA** is also easy to grow.

CRASSULA OVATA see Feng shui, page 91.

ECHEVERIA are mostly rosettes of bluey green leaves that send up spikes topped by bell-shaped flowers of orange, yellow and pink. EUPHORBIAS come in all sorts of shapes and sizes, many of them masquerading as cacti with spines. *E. obesa* is a squat round thing that looks like it's eaten too much and *E. millii*, the crown of thorns, has spiny stems with red or yellow flowers. GASTERIA VERRUCOSA has thick green leaves arranged in opposite pairs and covered in white warts and **HAWORTHIAS** are like aloes with banded and warty leaves. They don't need feeding. KALANCHOE BLOSSFELDIANA, see Unkillable, page 71. KALANCHOE DAIGREMONTIANA (*Bryophyllum daigremontianum*), the devil's backbone, can grow to about 90cm. The leaves are fringed with about 50 tiny plantlets that can be detached and potted up. LITHOPS are called living stones because the pairs of squat leaves 3 or 4cm wide look exactly like pebbles. In late summer a daisy flower grows from the slit between the leaves. They don't need feeding and shouldn't be watered between October and March.

SEDUM MORGANIANUM, the donkey's tail, is a fragile plant good for a hanging basket with its trailing stems of overlapping leaves. Sedums don't need feeding either. **SENECIO ARTICULATUS** is known as the hot dog plant because the stems look like pale grey sausages with a few leaves sprouting out the top. **SENECIO MACROGLOSSUS** is a trailing ivy-like plant with glossy variegated leaves.

TROUBLESHOOTING

- Wilting, saggy discoloured leaves and rots at the base of the plant are due to overwatering. Prune off any soft or rotted roots and propagate some new plants.
- Soft brown spots are signs of disease. Water with carbendazim.
- Brown spots on the leaves are caused by underwatering in summer.
- Flabby growth is a result of lack of light or excess water in winter.

AGAVES (left and below) prefer a cool room and like most succulents can be put outside in summer.

FERNS

Ferns are very primitive plants, probably only a nose ahead of mosses and lichens on the evolutionary scale. They don't flower, but to make up for this, they do have wonderful leaves, or fronds, which come in all sorts of weird shapes and sizes and some, like the Boston fern, are extremely good at purifying air and raising humidity. They are pretty easy to grow and will thrive in less light than many other indoor plants, but if you neglect them even briefly, they will get their own back by dying. Their big enemy is central heating which sucks all the humidity out of the air in the room. Keep the humidity high and you won't have problems.

SHORTCUTS TO SUCCESS
- Never let the compost dry out completely; some species will suffer badly if it happens even once.
- Keep the humidity up and keep plants away from radiators. • Don't put them in full sunshine or in total shade. • Watch out for scale and mealy bug. • Never use leafshine.

The **BOSTON FERN** (above left), drops its frondlets if humidity is low and watering uneven.
The **STAG HORN FERN** (above right) has antlers up to 80cm long covered in a white bloom. *Platycerium grande* is chunkier.
ATHYRIUM NIPPONICUM PICTUM (right) The Japanese painted fern has silvery markings like many Pteris.

FERNS

THE BASICS

Light The idea that ferns love deep shade is actually a fallacy. Good indirect average light is needed. Strong summer sun is dangerous so put ferns further back into the room or in an east- or north-facing window.

Temperature and humidity Normal room temperature is fine but the warmer it is, the more humidity is needed. Stand plants on a pebble tray and, if you can be bothered, mist daily. Low humidity causes brown frond tips. Bathrooms are good places for ferns.

Watering Never let the compost dry out ever. Water plentifully and keep it moist but not soggy. Ferns get through loads of water especially in higher temperatures.

Feeding Feed every two to three weeks during the active growth period with a liquid feed high in nitrogen. Always use it at half strength to avoid burning the delicate roots.

Potting and repotting Repot in spring when roots fill the pot. Most are shallow rooting so only use a half-depth pot and don't bury the crown. Use an equal mixture of peat substitute, leaf mould and perlite. Crunch up a piece of barbecue charcoal to keep the compost sweet. Plastic pots are better than porous terracotta.

Propagation Some ferns, like adiantum and cyrtomium, have underground rhizomes. Tease the plant apart and cut them into sections each with a frond or two. For plants with overground rhizomes, like phlebodium/polypodium and davallia, cut off the end 5cm of rhizome with or without leaves. Place in pots, peg down with a loop of wire and cover with a clear plastic bag for four weeks. Growing from spores is difficult, takes ages, so don't bother.

EASY-TO-GROW TYPES

BUTTON FERN, *Pellaea rotundifolia*, has pairs of dark green leathery leaflets on wiry stems and like the holly fern, *Cyrtomium falcatum*, doesn't suffer too much from lack of water and humidity.

RABBIT'S FOOT FERN, *Davallia canariensis*, has furry brown rhizomes that grow on the compost surface. If you underwater or it gets too cold, the triangular fronds drop off but will soon grow back.

THE BIRD'S NEST FERN, *Asplenium nidus*, makes a shuttlecock of upright, soft green shiny leaves that could happily reach 60cm tall indoors. Don't touch the young fronds as they unfurl or they'll get damaged. Excess heat makes leaf edges go black. Cut watering right down in winter. The appropriately named mother fern, *Asplenium bulbiferum*, has feathery fronds with tiny plantlets growing on the fringes. Pull them off and pot them up.

DICKSONIA SQUARROSA (above) need cool, bright rooms. Water the trunk as well as the pot.
HART'S TONGUE FERN (left) is very similar to a bird's nest fern, but less shiny.

BOSTON FERN, *Nephrolepis exaltata* 'Bostoniensis', makes a large mound of herringbone fronds as much as 60cm long and is probably one of the best ferns. *N. obliterata* is a bit tougher.

A BIT HARDER BUT STILL NOT VERY HARD

PTERIS suffer badly from lack of humidity and water especially if left in small pots in which they quickly dry out and die.

DICKSONIA SQUARROSA and other tree ferns can be kept in cool, bright rooms. Water the trunk so that it is constantly damp.

BLECHNUM FERN, *Blechnum gibbum*, needs the same treatment and makes a neat rosette of elegant fronds which eventually reach 90cm long.

HARE'S FOOT FERN, *Phlebodium/Polypodium aureum* 'Mandaianum', has really thick hairy rhizomes creeping on the compost surface and wonderful silvery blue fronds eventually reaching over 60cm tall. Grow in a wide shallow pot.

STAG'S HORN FERN, *Platycerium bifurcatum*, is one of the most prehistoric looking of the ferns and looks best fixed to a wall or in a hanging basket.

HART'S TONGUE FERN, *Phyllitis scolopendrium*, is like a smaller, more open bird's nest fern but with less shiny, wavy edged fronds. It's lovely anyway.

MAIDENHAIR FERN, the delicate Adiantum, has rightfully earned a place in the Challenging section (pages 73/75).

BULBS

An onion is a bulb. It's a fleshy food and water store that produces flowers and leaves for part of the year and then dies down and becomes a bulb again. There are some bulbs that remain evergreen all year but they're treated as indoor plants elsewhere in this book. Some of the plants here are technically corms or tubers but it all amounts to the same thing. For this book bulbs are divided into two groups – those that are really outdoor garden plants temporarily brought inside in pots and those which are a bit more tropical and need to be indoors all year.

OUTDOOR BULBS MOVED IN

Most of these garden bulbs are sold in autumn and generally flower the following spring. They're a good way to cheer up your room in winter and spring, and some are scented and make brilliant air fresheners. There are snowdrops, tulips, daffodils, crocus and dwarf iris in yellow, purple and blue. Hyacinths have a really strong sweet smell and come in white, pink, mauve and a blue one which looks like Marge Simpson's hairdo. There are also delicate little blue flowers such as scilla and muscari, the grape hyacinths.

The autumn crocus, colchicum, is pink or white and their brown corms will produce leafless flowers in autumn even if you don't plant them.

SHORTCUTS TO SUCCESS

- When buying make sure bulbs are firm and mould free.
- Always pick the shorter varieties of tulips and daffs or they'll flop over.
- Plant as soon as possible and keep moist.
- Once indoors keep as cool as possible and away from radiators.
- Put in a bright spot. Rotate pots every other day to stop bulb shoots bending towards the light.

THE BASICS

Plant bulbs in quite shallow compost, close together. Some bulbs, like the grape hyacinths, look fantastic in in a row of individual shot glasses. Put pots outside for the winter and bring them in just before the buds open. Larger bulbs like daffodils and hyacinths can be 'forced' or duped into flowering much earlier than normal. After planting they must be denied light and warmth. Bury the pots in a flower bed and cover them up with

Bring **BULBS** (above) into a cool room once the shoots are 4–5cm tall.
LILIES (left) have a beautiful perfume, but never flower as well in the second year (see Feng Shui).

155

about 15cm of moist peat substitute. Or put them in a black bag in a shed or garage. After eight or ten weeks, once the shoots are 4–5cm tall, bring them into a cool room at about 10°C. When they're ready to flower move to a bright window. The warmer the room, the quicker the flowers fade and die. Hyacinths can be bought 'prepared' so they flower particularly early.

If you haven't got anywhere outdoors to put your bulbs I'm afraid you're stuffed and will just have to buy potted, already shooting bulbs in the spring.

After they've flowered Cut off dead flower-heads and either plant bulbs outside immediately or just bung outside and leave in pots. The foliage will die down, the bulbs will dry out and they can be planted in the ground the following autumn. They can't be used indoors again.

INDOOR BULBS

These are ones that can't tolerate frost and so can't be kept outside in cold areas. They flower at different times throughout the year and are left in the pot when the foliage dies down, moved somewhere out of sight and kept cool and almost dry until they shoot up again the following season.

Amaryllis, or hippeastrum has big, sometimes vulgar trumpet flowers in spring, but they look amazing in bud as one or two phallic shoots arise from the bulb. *Gladiolus callianthus* 'Murielae', the Acidanthera is leagues ahead of ordinary gladioli with white, purple-hearted scented blooms in late summer. Canna lilies have bold, banana-like leaves in green to bronzy purple and large flowers of red, yellow or orange. The spider lily is found in gardens in the tropics and veltheimia is a good one for indoors, though the winter temperature must stay below 15°C.

SHORTCUTS TO SUCCESS

- Water only a little after planting the bulb.
- Step up watering once in leaf.
- Keep in bright light by a window while in flower and leaf.
- Keep in cool rooms if possible.

After they've flowered Cut off the flower when it fades but leave the stalk. Feed with liquid fertilizer after flowering every two weeks then switch to a high-potash, tomato feed until leaves wither. Keep quite dry once leaves have died down. Repot every three to four years.

ALLIUM (left), the ornamental onions, are best kept outside until their globes of flowers are actually open.

AMARYLLIS or **HIPPEASTRUM** (below) has big, sometimes vulgar, pink, white, orange or red trumpet flowers in spring. They look amazing in bud as one or two phallic shoots rise from the bulb.

CARNIVOROUS

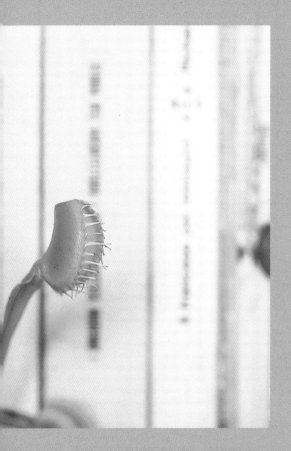

These easy-to-grow plants do actually eat insects. They live in places where nutrients are scarce so they've had to virtually give up on photosynthesis in favour of a more gruesome diet. Many are equipped with beautiful flowers, intricate patterns to lure their prey and cunning devices for trapping and killing. Victims are then dissolved in digestive juices leaving only the hard crunchy bits as evidence. Unfairly dismissed as novelty plants they are probably the most interesting indoor plants there are. Not only do they look good but they actually give you something back by keeping your house free of flies and mosquitoes and rid neighbouring indoor plants of aphids and whitefly. They are the height of organic pest control.

SHORTCUTS TO SUCCESS
- Always water with rainwater or defrosted freezer ice.
- Keep compost soggy in summer and moist in winter.
- Remove dead foliage as it dies down in winter.

THE BASICS
Water Hard or alkaline water is a killer so you must use rainwater, distilled water or defrosted freezer water. Just about all carnivorous plants need to have their feet wet during the spring to autumn growing season so stand them in a tray of 5cm of water. In winter all except the tropical species have a dormant period when plants form winter leaves. At this time let the saucer dry out before topping it up. This keeps the compost moist but not soggy.

Potting Generally they like an acidic peaty compost. Ironically their native habitats are being destroyed and drained for peat. To stop this gardeners should use peat substitutes (see Potting + Repotting, page 104). Individual requirements are listed for each plant. Premixed potting media are available from carnivorous plant specialists. When buying sphagnum moss check it is from a sustainable source. Plants won't need repotting for a year or two but when they do, put them into clay pots.

Light Give plenty of light. A south-facing window-sill is ideal, not least because they attract more flies than others. Conservatories and greenhouses are also good. Nepenthes and butterworts need a little shade but most hardy varieties can grow outside in sun.

VENUS FLY TRAPS (above) don't need any help from us as they catch enough flies on their own.
The **SUNDEWS** (right) have an incredibly sticky glob of glue on each of the tiny hairs. For small flies there's no escape.

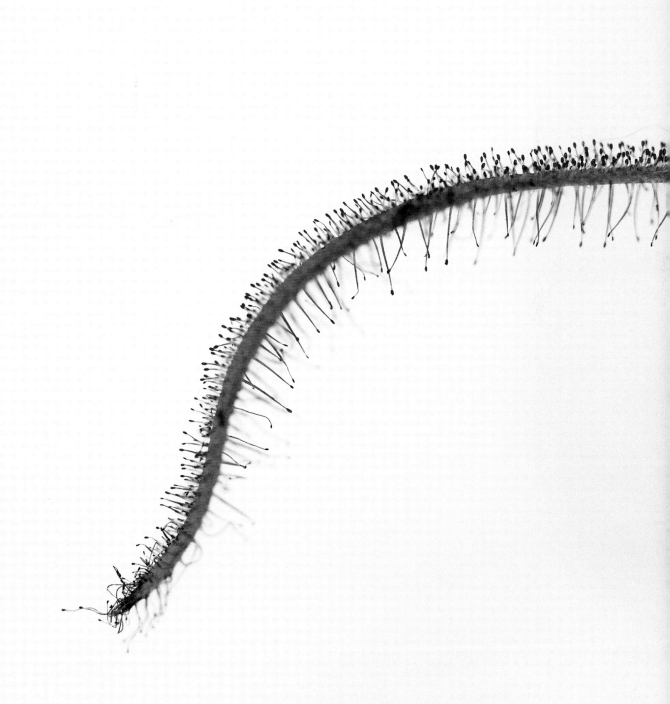

Feeding Of those listed here, only nepenthes ever need a fertilizer. All the others catch plenty of insects and don't need any help.

Temperature Normal room temperatures are fine for most from spring to autumn with a cooler winter temperature of about 4°C. This normally means a cold window-sill away from radiators or a cool, frost-free greenhouse or conservatory. In early spring move to a warmer spot and the plant will start growing new leaves. Plants can be put outside in summer, but they must be brought back inside in early autumn. Nepenthes favours warm rooms or greenhouses all year.

Pests and diseases Aphids can be a menace for some species and must be sprayed with a gentle organic insecticide like pyrethrum although butterworts and sundews catch small flying pests for themselves. Mealy bugs and scale should also be looked out for. Botrytis, the grey mould, can be a nuisance in autumn and winter particularly if you overwater. Remove any dead leaves as a matter of course, provide ventilation and spray with a systemic fungicide. Copper-based fungicides will kill your plants, so read labels carefully. If you put plants outside, smear the side of the saucer with grease to stop slugs and woodlice getting in.

VARIETIES

VENUS FLY TRAP, *Dionaea muscipula* from the USA is really easy to grow. An unsuspecting fly lands on the open trap, touches several of the trigger hairs in quick succession, and bang – the trap closes and the fly is caught behind bars. They don't need many flies to survive so don't try and feed them or artificially trigger the traps. Grow on a sunny window-sill, in temperatures up to 30°C in summer and down to 5°C in winter when they must have a rest. Cut off the flower stalks which weaken the plants and remove dead traps as they naturally die back. Grow in 70 per cent peat substitute, 30 per cent lime-free sand or perlite.

SUNDEWS, *Drosera*, have rosettes of flattened leaves covered in tiny, often red hairs tipped with an incredibly sticky glob of natural glue. Flies get stuck to the leaves which then actually fold over the victim and dissolve it. *Drosera capensis* is easy and the giant Australian fork-leaved sundews are brilliant mosquito catchers perfect for a hanging basket. Pot in 70 per cent peat substitute, 30 per cent lime-free sand.

PITCHER PLANTS, *Sarracenia*, are the most efficient traps there are, capturing hundreds of house flies, bluebottles and wasps. A slender trumpet draws insects with its beautifully patterned hood and the lure of nectar. The insect loses its footing and tumbles into the tube to be digested. The tubes may be richly variegated or coloured red or yellow and the usually solitary flowers are equally beautiful. *S. flava* has yellow hooded pitchers 50cm tall. Use 60 per cent peat substitute, 30 per cent lime-free sand, 10 per cent perlite.

TROPICAL PITCHER PLANTS, *Nepenthes*, are good for hanging baskets because the short, dumpy pitchers hang over the edge on tendrils. Bristles and a slippery wax around the mouth prevent escape and a fly is gone within a few hours. Nepenthes have no dormant period and need warm temperatures night and day, regular high nitrogen feeds and a high humidity. Pot in 50 per cent live sphagnum moss, 30 per cent perlite, 20 per cent small grade bark.

BUTTERWORT, *Pinguicula*, have a beautiful flower and form rosettes of pale leaves and look a little like starfish. The leaves feel like melted butter and this surface traps tiny flies and eats them. *P. vulgaris* is hardy and can be grown outside in a bog garden. Pot in 70 per cent peat substitute, 30 per cent lime-free horticultural sand.

BLADDERWORT, *Utricularia*. The aquatic species native to Britain floats in water so grow in a glass bowl. They have very cunning underwater traps which when triggered open a door and suck in their prey. Feed with live daphnia (water fleas) bought from a pet store. In winter they form resting buds and sink to the bottom.

Slit one of the beautiful **SARRACENIA** pitchers (left) lengthways and you'll find it stuffed full of flies.
The tropical pitcher plants, **NEPENTHES**, (below) need much warmer temperatures than most of the others.

CONSERVATORY

Whether you've got some sort of ramshackle glass lean-to or a state-of-the-art conservatory, you can use it to grow all kinds of fantastic plants. Things that just won't survive in the darker rooms of your home will thrive in the extra light levels and if you can heat it as well, the possibilities are endless. You can control the environment so it is actually more suited to plants than people and give them exactly what they want. Conservatories and greenhouses are usually either cool, warm or hot and it's mainly the temperature that dictates what plants you can grow.

THE TECHNICAL STUFF

Heating Unheated or cold greenhouses can be used to grow summer crops like tomatoes, overwinter tender plants and for propagation. But if you provide some form of heating your choice of plants is greater. Electric heaters with thermostats are the most reliable, efficient and convenient. Tubular heaters should be fixed to the wall just above the ground. Fan heaters can be moved around and create good air circulation providing an even temperature throughout and minimizing the spread of disease. Gas and paraffin heaters need good ventilation and aren't as good at regulating temperature. A maximum/minimum thermometer is essential for keeping an eye on things and a frost alarm which sounds indoors is useful to protect plants if there is a power cut or the fuel runs out.

Shading The high light levels make plants grow much faster than indoors so you'll probably have to do a lot more pruning. However, in summer, shading is particularly important on south-facing conservatories which can heat up very quickly and cause a lot of damage to plants. Sun-tolerant climbers grown under the roof provide natural shading to plants beneath and spraying a shading paint onto the glass is a practical but messy option for greenhouses. Otherwise blinds are the best solution. A cheap alternative is to buy rolls of hessian from a builders' merchant or upholsterers and staple gun it to the wooden glazing bars of the roof. In winter, on the other hand, some plants, particularly those from the southern hemisphere need as much light as possible and can even benefit from extra artificial light (see Light and Artificial Light, page 95).

Humidity The air can get far too hot and dry in summer so you'll need to raise the humidity to keep the plants happy. Each day, close all the doors

GLORIOSA SUPERBA (above) The glory lily grows to about 1.2m and must be kept dry in winter.
TIBOUCHINA GRANDIFOLIA (left) The purple glory bush needs lots of winter sunlight.

163

and windows for an hour or so and water the floor. As it evaporates the humidity dramatically increases which also keeps the dreaded red spider mite at bay. If you haven't got a wettable tiled floor place trays of water amongst the plants or purchase an electric humidifier. In winter, excess humidity is the problem.

Ventilation This is really important, even in cold greenhouses, to avoid a build-up of damp, stale air and to regulate temperature. In summer, doors and windows should be opened to cool the place down. Automatic openers can be fitted to vents, and kitchen and bathroom extractor fans controlled by thermostat are ideal.

Pests and diseases In an enclosed environment pests and diseases multiply and spread with the alarming rate of a biblical plague. Once established, infestations are hard to control so you have to be ever vigilant and stamp out problems as soon as you spot them. When bringing in new plants you should examine them minutely and, if possible, quarantine them for a month.

Introducing biological controls of insect predators, parasites and pathogens to conservatories can keep pests to a manageable level. But they are most successful in warmer temperatures and don't work so well in winter months (see page 99). Sometimes prevention is better than cure. Vine-weevil attacking nematodes can be introduced in August and September, and leaf pests can be kept at bay by routinely spraying with insecticidal soap every few weeks.

HOW WARM?

Cool Heated to about 2°C, just enough to keep it above freezing, you can overwinter tender garden plants and grow all sorts of exotic things. Many will even put up with an occasional frost, particularly if kept fairly dry at the roots and fed with a high-potassium fertilizer in late summer. The minimum daytime temperature should be between 5–10°C. Suitable climbers include *Plumbago capensis* with its powder-blue flowers, *Lapageria*, the Chilean bellflower, various passion flowers, jasmines and edible grapes. Flowering plants like pelargoniums, fuchsias, abutilon and salvias will thrive, and tender exotics like bottlebrush, ginger, palms and oleander will all be happy.

Warm Daytime temperature should be around 14°C dropping to a minimum 8°C at night. In summer you need to keep the humidity up. You can grow lots of the ordinary indoor plants listed elsewhere in this book but check the temperature requirements first.

Allamanda cathartica is a great climber for creating shade and produces lots of large yellow flowers for most of the year. It needs cutting back by a third each spring. The bizarre flowered heliconia will grow here, but needs a cooler winter rest. The deliciously scented frangipani, *Plumeria*, will make a large bush and the bird of paradise, *Strelitzia reginae*, with its orange and blue bird-like flowers will thrive. Citrus will also do well as will lots

The **LOBSTER CLAW** (right), heliconia, is a banana-like plant, reaching several metres high.
CUPHEA IGNEA (below left) The cigar plant and its purple-flowered relative are covered in flowers for most of the year.
ALLAMANDA (below right) The golden trumpet grows quickly and needs cutting back annually by a third.

of palms, certain orchids and that familiar plant of the Mediterranean, bougainvillea with its masses of papery, pinky purple flowers. *Tibouchina urvilleana*, with its big saucer-shaped purple flowers in summer and autumn, will grow into a large bush, but is prone to red spider mite, as are most conservatory plants – check under the velvety leaves. Feed monthly and keep fairly dry in winter. *Cuphea ignea*, the cigar plant and its purple-flowered relative, are covered in flowers most of the year. Leaf edges turn red in plenty of sun.

Hot These are truly tropical conditions with a minimum of about 20°C that let you grow some of the familiar indoor plants and plenty of things that would never succeed in your living room. The humidity must be kept high with the raised temperatures and it can get a bit sweaty for people. Indoor swimming pools usually fall into this range. Plants keep growing all year so you must continue watering and feeding.

Banana plants will fruit at this temperature, plenty of bromeliads, ferns and orchids will thrive along with tropical cycads and palms. The glory lily, *Gloriosa superba* carries red and yellow flowers in summer and autumn and grows to about 1.2m high. It needs full light and plenty of watering and feeding once growth begins, but dies down in winter, when watering should be stopped. All parts of the plant are highly poisonous and handling the tubers can irritate the skin, so wear gloves. *Heliconia rostrata*, the lobster claw, needs to be fed monthly, watered freely, and should be grown in sandy or gritty soil in plenty of light, but not direct sun.

OUTSIDE IN

Take a look in your local garden centre and it won't take long to realize that there are far more garden plants for sale than there are indoor plants. It seems a shame not to exploit this and there's no reason why you can't bring all sorts of garden plants into your home for a few days or even weeks. But instead of being binned afterwards, they can be put outside where they'll live to fight another day. Horticultural purists will probably want to have you flogged, but it's healthy to break a few rules now and again.

WHAT PLANTS ARE GOOD?
Scented and flowering plants are particularly worthwhile and containerized trees straight from the garden centre can be quite dramatic. In theory you can use anything but plants with thick glossy leaves, like laurel, tend to put up with indoor conditions for a bit longer than plants with soft, thin leaves.

Other things like agapanthus, which you couldn't possibly grow inside, can be kept in pots and brought in when they're in flower and put back out to recover when they've finished. But you can't just dig up plants to bring them in, they must live in pots all year round.

The **STAR JASMINE**, *Trachelospermum jasminoides*, (above) can be brought inside for two or three weeks in a cool room.
The fragrant flowers of **SKIMMIA** (right) will last for about two weeks indoors.

OUTSIDE IN

SHORTCUTS TO SUCCESS
- Check for bugs beforehand.
- Avoid really warm rooms.
- Place near windows in lots of light.
- Always keep the compost moist.
- Watch the plants for signs of distress.
- Rotate plants almost daily so all sides get some light.
- Only keep indoors for a short time, don't torture them.
- Don't bring the same plant in two years in a row.
- Put plants back outside into some shade at first.

WHEN CAN YOU BRING THEM IN?

If it's only for a really short time, perhaps a matter of days, then you can bring a plant indoors virtually whenever you fancy it as long as you follow the shortcuts. For longer stays, the time of year that you bring plants in is really important. If you take in a deciduous tree or shrub in winter, for example, the warmth of your home will force it into leaf prematurely and then when you put it outside, the cold weather could kill all the buds and maybe the whole plant. The extremes of temperature are what are most likely to make the plants suffer. In summer it's not so bad because the temperature of your home isn't going to be a great deal warmer than outside and may even be cooler. Remember this is only a temporary exercise and that even if they look fine, garden plants will start to get stressed out as soon as they enter your home.

Ideally you need a garden or some sort of outdoor space so you can move things in and out as you please and then let them recover outside for a year or two. It's best to give plants a bit of time off before bringing them in again.

Always check plants thoroughly for pests and diseases. You don't want slugs and woodlice running around your carpet and things like aphids and vine weevil will happily set up home on your ordinary indoor plants. The cosy environment of your living room could even cause a population explosion. If possible, slip the pot off and cast your eye over the compost.

Spring In early spring deciduous trees and bushes with interesting bark make really different indoor plants. Silver birch, willows and the red-stemmed dogwoods are particularly good. All are likely to come into leaf and should be protected from frosts once they're put outside or they may suffer as a result. Clipped topiary of box and lonicera will also do well in cool rooms. There are scented shrubs like the Mexican orange blossom with its white flowers and

CORDYLINE AUSTRALIS (above) will last for several months in a cool room in winter, but needs high light levels in summer. AGAVE AMERICANA (left) can be brought into a cool, bright room in winter, but watch out for the spines.

aromatic green leaves, and *Skimmia japonica* will fill a whole room with its sweet smell which is wasted outdoors in late spring. Exochorda and *Spiraea* 'Arguta' are absolutely clothed in white blossom and will really bring the excitement of spring indoors.

Summer All through summer there are heaps of perennial plants that can be brought in for a few days: aconite, columbine, cosmos, day lilies, osteospermum, cone flowers, chrysanthemum and crocosmia. Experiment with anything you like. Bamboos can mostly be brought in, but the low light levels will eventually be a problem. Keep watered well and if the leaves show any sign of curling rush them back outside. Other candidates are buddleia, ornamental grasses, liriope, mock orange, lavender, laburnum, and climbers like

the star jasmine, *Trachelospermum jasminoides* and wisteria.

Autumn Apart from flowering shrubs like hydrangea there are plants with autumn colour as well. The hardy plumbago, ceratostigma, goes bright red and then there are trees like *Sorbus aucuparia* with red berries. As autumn progresses, frost-tender palms can be brought into cool, bright rooms.

Winter There are a number of shrubs which often have scented flowers on bare stems in winter like chimonanthus, corylus, corylopsis, hamamelis and *viburnum fragrans*. The conifers with needles like pines and spruces will survive a few weeks indoors in winter but those with flat leaves like chamaecyparis and thuja will probably die but it won't be obvious for months.

169

BUYER'S GUIDE

An unhealthy indoor plant is a sad, depressing creature and should be avoided at all costs. Most of the time, plants offered for sale by shops and nurseries are perfectly healthy. But there are a few caveats to observe to make sure you're not buying one which has already had its death warrant signed and that isn't going to infect and kill any plants you already have. If you get something that's been suffering since before you parted with any cash, that plant is going to struggle from day one, no matter how green-fingered you are and, if it's diseased or infected, it will spread to everything else.

WHERE TO BUY?

Markets can be very cheap places to buy plants, but in winter the plants may suffer from being outside in the cold. Shops are okay but they are often darker than they should be and if indoor plants are put out on the pavement in all weathers they can get bashed around in the process and scorched by the chilling winds. They may look fine when you hand over the money but when you get them home the damage starts to show up. It's pot luck when it comes to supermarkets and DIY warehouses, so garden centres and nurseries are usually your best bet.

CHOOSING A HEALTHY PLANT

Check out the nursery or shop. It should be clean and tidy because hygiene is really important to plant health. If there are fallen leaves and flowers around this is very bad news as bugs and diseases will probably be lurking amongst them. I'm not suggesting an official tour around with a clip board, a casual glance should be enough, but if the place is a mess then the plants are less likely to be in fine fettle. You should probably leave immediately.

If your chosen vendor passes the first test you need to look at the plants themselves. Stick your finger into the compost; well looked after plants should generally be moist. If it's very soggy or very dry this may be bad news, unless of course the plants specifically need those conditions. A crusty whiteness on the surface of the compost or the side of clay pots is a tell-tale sign of incorrect feeding. That certainly isn't the end of the world but it helps to build up an overall picture.

If you find something you like, look to see if there are other plants the same. Retailers normally buy in batches and it's nice to have a few to compare it with. If it's on its lonesome there's every chance it's the worst of the bunch and may have been kicking around for some time.

A plant should generally look healthy without damaged or discoloured leaves or broken branches. If you're buying a flowering plant, try and get one with buds that are about to open but if it's in flower already check that there are still more to come.

Once you've chosen a plant, inspect it meticulously for pests and diseases – this is the single most important thing you must do. Look very closely under the leaves, on the shoot tips and where the leaves join the stems. Search for tiny whiteflies, brown scales, little bits of white fluff, tiny cobwebs and fine grey furry mould. Any suspicions and you should walk away. White blotches on the surface of the leaves is usually a harmless residue from watering, just check that it easily rubs off with your thumb. Next, when the shopkeeper isn't looking, give the plant a gentle shake to see if any leaves fall off – this is a bad sign.

THE JOURNEY BACK

Finally, you need to get your immaculate plant home safely. Make sure fragile specimens are really carefully wrapped and, if you're putting one in a car, get someone to hold it or wedge it in really well. It only has to fall over once to be spoiled. The most important thing is not to expose it to wind so you should keep the windows shut and if you're going on public transport make sure all the leaves are covered up. If you've bought a big plant you'll be tempted to stick it out through the sunroof but this is very dangerous. As you drive home the plant will be subjected to the equivalent of gale force winds, all the leaves will get damaged and the plant will probably die.

A NEW HOME

Some plants get a real shock when you take them out of their cosy home and put them into your own. Some, like the familiar weeping fig, start to drop their leaves but they normally grow back. Try to acclimatize plants slowly and don't subject them to a massive change in temperature. Avoid draughts and if a plant has been grown in lots of light, start it off near the window before inching it back into the room over the course of several weeks.

SUPPLIERS

PLANTS

BONSAI
Bushukan Bonsai
Ricbra, Lower Road,
Hockley, Essex SS5 5NL
Tel 01702 201029
Fax 01702 200657

BROMELIADS + INDOOR FERNS
Newington Nurseries
Newington, near
Stadhampton,
Oxon OX10 7AW
Tel 01865 400533
Fax 01865 891766
www.newington-
nurseries.co.uk

British Pteridological
Society
www.nhm.ac.uk/hosted_si
tes/bps/index.htm

BULBS
The International Bulb
Society
www.bulbsociety.com

P. De Jager & Sons
The Nurseries, Marden
Kent TN12 9BP
tel 01622 831235
fax 01622 832416
PdeJag@aol.com

CACTI + SUCCULENTS
British Cactus and
Succulent Society
http://cactus-mall.com/bcss

Brookside Nursery
Elderberry Farm
Bognor Rd, Rowhook,
Horsham,
West Sussex RH12 3PS
Tel 01403 790996
Fax 01403 790195

Southfield Nurseries
Bourne Rd, Morton, Bourne,
Lincs PE10 0RH
Tel 01778 570168

CARNIVOROUS
Carnivorous Plant
Society
66 Pine Crescent,
Hutton, Brentwood,
Essex CM13 1JB

Hampshire Carnivorous
Plants
Ya-Mayla, Allington Lane,
West End, Southampton,
Hants SO30 3HQ
Tel 023 8047 3314
Fax 023 8047 3314

CITRUS
The Citrus Centre
West Mare Lane,
Pulborough,
West Sussex RH20 2EA
Tel 01798 872786
www.citruscentre.co.uk

CONSERVATORY
The Palm Centre Ltd
Ham Central Nursery,
Ham Street,
Ham, Richmond,
Surrey TW10 7HA
Tel 020 8255 6191
Fax 020 8255 6192

The Conservatory
Station Road,
Gomshall,
Surrey GU5 9LB
Tel/Fax 01483 203019
www.conservatoryplants.com

Fleur de Lys
Restharrow Cottage,
Lower Street,
Fittleworth,
West Sussex RH20 1EL
Tel 01798 865475
Fax 01798 865475

HERBS + VEGETABLES
The Herb Society
Deddington Hill Farm,
Warmington, Banbury,
Oxon OX17 1XB
www.herbsociety.co.uk

ORCHIDS
The Orchid Society of
Great Britain
Athelney,
145 Binscombe Village,
Godalming,
Surrey GU7 3QL
Tel/Fax 01483 421423

Burnham Nurseries
Forches Cross,
Newton Abbot,
Devon TQ12 6PZ
Tel 01626 352233
Fax 01626 362167

ORGANIC HERBS + VEGETABLES
Jekka's Herb Farm
Rose Cottage,
Shellards Lane,
Allveston,
Bristol BS35 3SY
Tel 01454 418878
Fax 01454 411988
farm@jekkasherbfarm.com
www.jekkasherb.com.demon.
co.uk

WHEATGRASS
Wheatgrass juicer
www.discountjuicers.com/
wheatgrass.html

Wheatgrass Seed
www.wheatgrasskits.com

BUYING PLANTS FROM ABROAD
Ministry of Agriculture,
Fisheries and Food
Plant Health Division,
Foss House,
King's Pool,
1–2 Peasholme Green,
York YO1 7PX
Tel 44(0) 1904 45
5191/5192/5195
Fax 44(0) 1904 45 5199
q.info@ph.maff.gsi.gov.uk

SEEDS
Chiltern Seeds
Bortree Stile, Ulverston,
Cumbria LA12 7PB
Tel 01229 581137 (24hr)
Fax 01229 584549
info@chilternseeds.co.uk
www.chilternseeds.co.uk

Thompson & Morgan
Poplar lane, Ipswich,
Suffolk 1P8 3BU
Tel 01473 688821
Fax 01473 680199
Tmuk@thompson-
morgan.com
www.thompson-
morgan.com

Mr. Fothergill's Seeds Ltd
Newmarket,
Suffolk CB8 7QB
Tel 01638 552512
Mailorder@mr-
forthergills.co.uk

FENG SHUI
Feng Shui Association
31 Woburn Place,
Brighton BN1 9GA
Tel/fax 01273 693844
www.fengshuiassociation.
co.uk

ARTIFICIAL LIGHT
Philips Lighting Ltd
The Philips Centre,
420–430 London Rd,
Croydon CR9 3QR
Tel 020 8665 6655
www.philips.com

FERTILISER, INSECTICIDES + COMPOSTS
The Scotts Co (UK) Ltd
Salisbury House,
Weyside Park,
Catteshall Lane,
Godalming,
Surrey GU7 1XE
Tel 01483 410210
Fax 01483 410220
www.scotts.co.uk

Scotts (Levingtons)
Advice Line
0500 888558

Chase Organics
River Dene Business Park,
Molesey Rd, Hersham
Surrey KT12 4RG

BIOLOGICAL CONTROL
Hendry Doubleday
Research Association
Ryton Organics Gardens,
Coventry CV8 3LG
Tel 024 7630 3517
Fax 024 7663 9229
enquiry@hdra.org.uk

Defenders Ltd
Occupation Rd,
Wye, Ashford,
Kent TN25 5EN
Tel 01233 813121

CERAMIC POTS
Pret-a-Pot
6a Cow Lane,
Sidlesham, Chichester,
West Sussex PO20 7LN
Tel 01243 641928
Fax 01243 641945
enquiries@pret-a-pot.com
www.pret-a-pot.com

HYDROPONICS
Greenfinger
Hydroponics
182 Hook Rd,
Tolworth, Surbiton,
Surrey KT6 5BZ
tel 020 8255 8999
or 2 Jowett Street
Peckham, London
SE15 6JN
Tel 020 7708 4999
puddle@vanoord.u-net.com

INDEX